Vanishing
Ireland

VANISHING IRELAND

James Fennell & Turtle Bunbury

HODDER
HEADLINE
IRELAND

First published in 2006 by Hodder Headline Ireland

1

A CIP catalogue record for this title is available from the British Library.

ISBN 0340 92277 X
ISBN 978 0340 92277 4

Typeset in Garamond by Anú Design, Tara
Cover and text design by Anú Design, Tara
Printed and bound in Great Britain by Butler & Tanner, Frome

Hodder Headline Ireland's policy is to use papers that are natural, renewable and recyclable products and made from
wood grown in sustainable forests. The logging and manufacturing processes are expected to conform to the
environmental regulations of the country of origin.

Hodder Headline Ireland
8 Castlecourt Centre
Castleknock
Dublin 15
Ireland

A division of Hodder Headline, 338 Euston Road, London NW1 3BH, England

CONTENTS

This book is dedicated to our beautiful brides,
Joanna Fennell and Ally Bunbury

It is also for the amazing Betty Scott whose conversations over decades past
proved to be the inspiration behind the Vanishing Ireland project.

And a special thank you to Wendy Walsh
who made the making of this book possible.

INTRODUCTION

They say that when Zeus is deposed, chaos reigns. Ireland in the twenty-first century is a country that has much to come to terms with. In the last twenty years, the pace of life has accelerated to such an astonishing degree that even children agree time is flying. In the 1990s, we witnessed the country's Roman Catholic Church tumble from its lofty heights. At the same time, we found ourselves in the utterly unexpected position of becoming a prosperous country. There may be talk of golden ages in Irish history but the common people of Ireland had never experienced them. Very suddenly, everything changed. By the year 2000, most young people were earning enough money to invest in houses, cars and leisurely holidays. The mass emigration of the Irish to foreign shores, a constant for over three centuries, came to an abrupt halt. Indeed, there was much about the past that now seemed irrelevant.

However, throughout this island there are men and women whose traditional ways do not sit quite so easily with this brave new Ireland. To younger generations, their sepia-hued world is difficult to comprehend. It seems like an almost make-believe land of thatched cottages, potato furrows and pony traps. The stage on which these tribal elders played out their lives was little different to that of their grandparents before them. And, of course, it was every bit as real as our own.

Posterity does not generally acknowledge the common people as anything more than an electoral statistic. Their life stories have always faded into the archives. This book sets out to capture and preserve the stories of some of these people. When they were children, Ireland was one of the poorest countries in Europe. Their parents were adults during the horrific days of the First World War and the Irish Civil War. Their grandparents may have remembered the Great Famine of the 1840s. The grandfather of one man we met knew people who fought in the 1798 Rebellion. History can play strange tricks with time.

Some people don't like looking back at the past. Spike Milligan famously declared that it hurt his neck. The older generation?? here lived through remarkable and difficult times. The Ireland of their youth allowed for little optimism. As children, many of those we met had slept in the same beds as their siblings, walked to school barefoot and fed on cabbage and potatoes and perhaps some of the salty bacon

hanging from the kitchen ceiling. Their homes had no electricity, no running water, no washing machine, no fridge, no television, no telephones. Families were large, the number of children often running into double figures. Fathers generally walked or cycled to work. Most had a donkey or horse which they'd hitch to a trap if need be. Farmers conglomerated at the weekly cattle and sheep fairs. Social life revolved around mass, always an excellent place for picking up the latest gossip. Some followed the hunt, others preferred the giddy fiddles and dancing feet of the céilís. The postman occasionally brought word from aunts, uncles, brothers and sisters, who had left home to make a new life in England or America. For many who stayed behind, alcohol afforded an emigration for the soul. Others took the pledge and never touched a drop. Curiously, most of them insist that, despite everything, the Ireland of their youth was a better place. As Atty Dowling told us, 'O God it was a hard life – but it was a grand life. And whatever the hell way it was, the people was somehow happier and more contented.'

In the present century, Church authority has all but collapsed. Politics is following fashion onto the catwalk. Rural villages have been smothered in suburbs. Farming is no longer a simple collaboration between man, beast and soil. It is a highly complex financial industry orchestrated by anonymous bureaucrats in Brussels.

But change is constant. The trusty horse was a vital cog on the Irish farm since Celtic times. After the Second World War, the tractor arrived and farm-horses suddenly became redundant. During the late nineteenth century, the railway and the canals were the principal forms of transport. By 1960, both had been cast aside to make way for the car. Today, we watch as vast swathes of the landscape, each inch soaked in history, are cleared to make way for the super highways and urban sprawl of the present age.

The people we met in the making of this book were invariably charming, courteous, amusing and friendly. Some were eloquent, others indecipherable. Some hardly said a word. One or two didn't stop to draw breath. Some spoke profound truisms that no philosopher has yet considered. Others invented everything as they went along. They all completely understood the nature of this project, plying us with tea and whiskey while they coloured in the past with their memories and mused upon the quandaries of the present. There is nothing quite like watching the eyes of an ancient light up beneath his peaky cap as he recalls a punchline from long ago that leaves him with no option but to laugh and laugh until the tears come gently rolling down his cheeks.

Ireland has inevitably become a more stressful and a less friendly society since the economic boom began. Ninety-three-year-old Ginger Pole genially says that it is nobody's fault and if he were young, he'd be exactly the same. Perhaps it's simply a consequence of the global culture making the world a smaller place. In the age of emails and mobile phones, you're less compelled to communicate with your neighbours. There's no need to even know their names. And now the smoking ban, rising prices and the clamp down on drink-driving means that even the country pub is in danger of extinction. The arrival of nearly half a million non-nationals to Ireland in recent years will invite further cause for contemplation in coming decades.

The Republic of Ireland's population currently stands at 4.2 million, its highest level since records began in 1861. About ten per cent of our population are over seventy years old, with most of them living in rural areas. People are living longer; there are presently 141 centenarians in the country, two of whom feature in these pages. But the generation who knew Ireland in the 1920s and 1930s are rapidly disappearing. The days of the 'golden codger', as W. B. Yeats once called them, will soon be at an end. They are dying off, fading out, literally vanishing from this earth. At the time of writing, six of those interviewed for this book have passed on. It is a simple and rather poignant truth that within the next decade – or, at most, two – we will look back and wonder where did all the golden codgers go?

Turtle Bunbury
August 2006

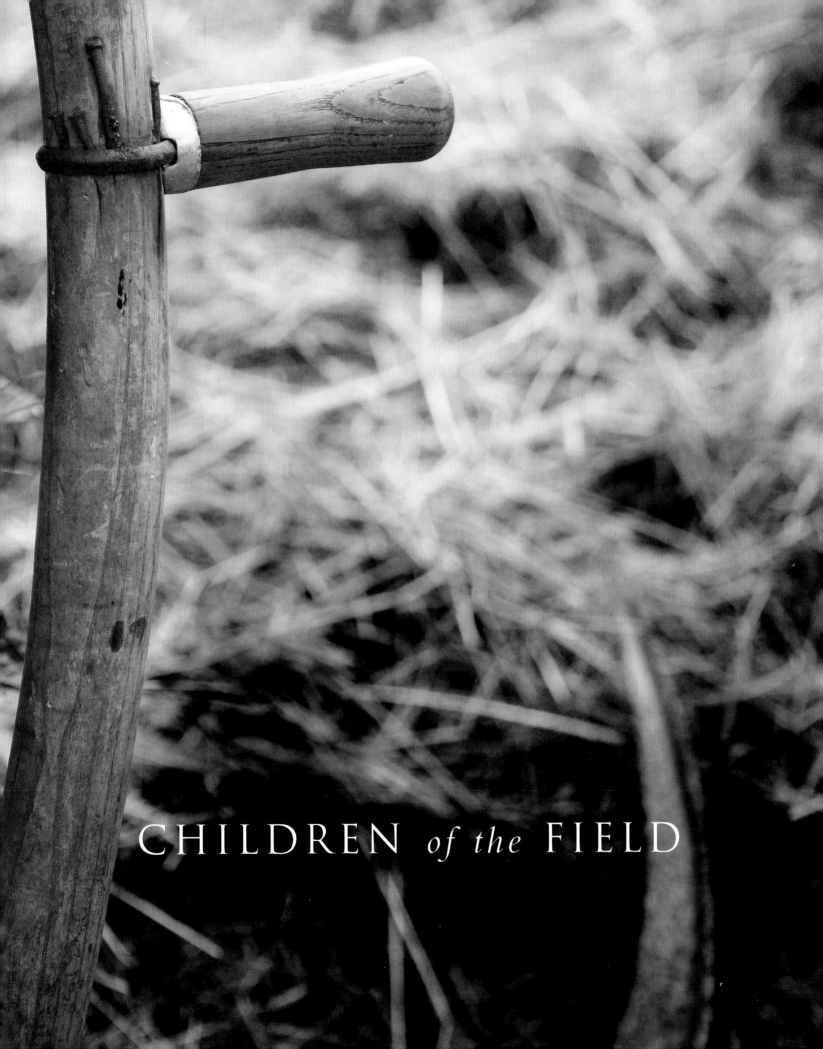

CHILDREN *of the* FIELD

PADDY GLEESON

Born 1904

Farmer

Kealderra, near Bodyke, East Clare

Paddy Gleeson is one of those remarkable characters who makes the rigid timelines of the past just fall away. He is a 103-year-old bachelor farmer living on his own in an old stone cottage in east Clare.

Paddy was a teenager during the First World War. One of his earliest memories is of the redoubtable Willie Redmond then MP for east Clare, arriving in the county in August 1914 to raise a regiment of Volunteers to help the Belgians fight the Germans. Redmond brought with him a fine banner under which he hoped the men would rally. 'It was a beautiful flag, green blazes with a harp at its centre,' recalls Paddy. 'There were scores of dummy rifles too, for training. But there was big opposition to the British government in the Church and everywhere.' Redmond abandoned his mission and went to France where he was killed at Messines in 1917. But the banner he brought to Clare stayed in the county and that, says Paddy, 'is the how and the why of Clare getting the name of the Banner County'.

The Gleeson family were cattle farmers from Sixmilebridge. 'My grandfather was born just after the Famine.' At the turn of the century, Paddy's father, Bartholomew, took on the pub at the O'Callaghan Mills. In a short space of time, he married the mill owner's daughter and, on 20 May 1904, Paddy was born where Doyle's Pub is today. He was followed by four siblings before his mother died in 1911. 'I was nine years old when she left us, with a baby sister and all.'

Money was scarce but, the outbreak of war in 1914, brought greater hardship. In October 1916, Bartholomew sold the pub and moved to New York with his two younger sons and a daughter. Paddy, by now fourteen years old, was left behind with his other sister to look after an elderly aunt. 'She had no one to care for her so I stopped here. Otherwise I would have gone out to the brothers.' The aunt proved to be a great teacher. 'She said you should always try and come out the same door you went in.'

'I never saw him again after that,' says Paddy of his father. 'He died there and is buried there. But,' he adds with a broad smile, 'I have seen the Statue of Liberty.' In the 1960s, Paddy flew to America for a reunion with 'the brothers'. They showed him Wall Street, the United Nations and the Westpoint Academy. At the latter, he came upon a monument to all the Irish who died in the American Civil War. 'I got the surprise of my life to see all these local names I was used to seeing here at home.'

Paddy says Clare had a rough time of it in the lead up to independence. Food and money were scarce, emigration was high and evictions were rampant. The people still remembered the events at Bodyke in June 1887 when the McNamara family fought back against their evictors with boiling water and hives of bees.

In Paddy's youth, resistance remained strong. 'Once, I was coming to school and I met two fellows leading a three-year-old bullock with horns. On his horns was a placard – 'The Land for the People and the Road for the Bullock'. And beneath the bull, they were dragging a man who was after evicting a poor widow woman from her home.' The widow's home had been knocked but 'the local people seen how fast it takes to build a house but they did it faster. She was evicted at ten in the morning and she was inside a house that night they built for her in the day! Timber and galvanised!'

Paddy recalls de Valera addressing the crowd in the by-election that followed Redmond's death. To the surprise of many, the people of Clare elected 'Dev' to Westminster by a majority of 2,975 votes. He would go on to represent the constituency until 1959. But Dev was in America when, in January 1920, Lloyd-George's Coalition dispatched the notorious Black and Tans to Ireland.

East Clare was one of the areas worst affected by the violent activity of these mercenaries. 'All around east Clare they were every day out searching for people and burning houses. They were an awful shower. A lot of them were jailbirds. They were sent over here to do the damage.'

Paddy was making his way home from the village with groceries one evening when he saw a Tan convoy of motorcycles and Crossley Tenders parked outside the home of his neighbours, the Hogans. 'There must have been twenty of them or more. Black hats, tan coat. I hid up an ivy tree and I was there from seven o'clock to eleven o'clock with my bag of groceries. That was 19 December 1920. I heard them going and I went over to the house and everything was upside down.' By the time Paddy got home, the Tans were raiding the house next door to his aunt. They came back again the following night. 'They had the mother and daughter brought out of the building wearing only their nightclothes. Then they set fire to the house. We heard them going and went over to see could we do anything. At that time, farmers used to kill their own pigs and store them in a barrel to season. I saved that and I saved chairs and I even saved the duck eggs. But the house was burned to the ground.'

'So here I am,' he says matter-of-factly. He may be 'facing 104' as he puts it, but he's looking good for a few more years yet. Over thirty full moons have already waxed and waned since President McAleese sent him a Centenarian's Medal in May 2004. Inscribed on the medal is Patrick Kavanagh's plea to the aged, 'Tell Us What Life has Taught You'. On the same occasion, nine-year-old Eoin McGrath wrote him a birthday card. 'You have seen many things in your life from World War One to the Millennium. You must have had an interesting life.'

It is difficult to know the secret of Paddy's longevity – it's hardly the Silk Cut cigarettes he puffs. Although born in a pub, he doesn't really drink so that might have helped. He never married either – 'although maybe I'll meet someone my age soon'.

STEPHEN JOHN TIERNEY

Born 1935

Farmer

Lough Corrib, County Galway

Stephen John Tierney is a Corribean. At least, that is what some call those who live along the shores of the majestic Lough Corrib in County Galway. His home lies in the wet and rocky high ground just north of Oughterard, a stone's throw from the sumptuous Victorian manor house hotel of Currarevagh. Indeed, the cottage where he and his wife live, used to be Currarevagh's laundry house.

Stephen John's family has worked with Currarevagh since the nineteenth century. An uncle was coachman to the estate's former owner, Mr Oliver, but when the landlord died on Christmas Day 1914, 'that was the end of my uncle's time'. The redundant coachman sailed for America but was soon drafted into the army and sent back to Europe to fight in the First World War. Three weeks later, he was wounded in action and that gave him a pension for life. 'He said the war was the best thing that ever happened to him,' chuckles his nephew.

The oldest of ten children, Stephen John has run a fifty-acre cattle farm for most of his life, though he would not expect his sons to follow in his footsteps. 'Make a living on it if you can and if you can't, pack it up. Farms are a thing of the past,' he maintains, 'and all that's keeping them going are old lads like me at seventy! A young lad doesn't want to know about it.'

He is a very well-read man, as at home with Shakespeare and current affairs as he is with Maurice Semple's local history. 'I read every sort of book that ever existed,' he says. Such devotion is perhaps a compensation for having to leave school young. He had not wanted to leave but 'the teacher never got a bob for teaching you after you were fourteen so, man or woman, out the door you went once you're fourteen'. By a series of coincidences, he was actually the only child in his class for the last four months of his schooldays. As such, he effectively became a servant to the teacher, 'an old man, born in America of Irish parents'. 'All I ever did was go down and post letters for the teacher, get the paper for him, get meat in the butcher's shop and all this sort of thing.'

When electricity arrived in Lough Corrib in 1954, Stephen John recalls passing houses where 'old lads would say, "There's nothing like that coming in here – that's pure witchcraft."' Likewise, the 'voices' unleashed by the electric wireless provoked a major outcry. 'People had an idea these things weren't good

for you,' he says, 'but by the time the television came, they were used to it.' Stephen John though, has little patience for superstitions. He recalls a story his grandfather told about the funeral of the Reverend Alexander Dallas, a controversial Protestant clergyman who ran a soup kitchen along the lake shore during the Great Famine. His grandfather told him that 'a flash of lightning lifted Dallas up out of the bed'. Stephen John regards this as 'codology of the highest order'. 'It's lunatic's talk – if lightning lifted him out of the bed, it would have smashed the house to pieces.'

Besides which, you don't need to make things up to have a good story. He lights a Gold Flake cigarette and recalls a friend who happened to be night watchman for 'a gang of poitín makers' on one of Lough Corrib's islands. The police were 'dead down' on poitín at this time and one night made an undercover raid and caught everyone, bar Tom. 'Now Tom was guilty of nothing,' counsels Stephen John. 'But he was the watchout – and he was the best man in Ireland to bring you a bottle of poitín if you wanted one.' Tom was on the run for three months before a squad car chanced upon him. As it happened, he had two bottles of poitín secreted in his pockets, a gift for an old couple in Oughterard. 'Now if you ever heard of a man with nerves of steel,' marvels Stephen John, 'this was him.' Tom was brought into the barracks and sat down in front of seven officers. He was interrogated and cross-examined and eventually asked to sign 'a heap of literature'. 'Tom stooped down and the top of one of the bottles came up and out. Tom's breath froze as he signed his name quick as a flash and straightened up again – they never seen it! Tom duly left the barracks, a free man. He walked a hundred yards before his two legs started to go with the fear.' And that, says Stephen John, is 'a very fact'.

HENRY CHAPMAN & RED TOM

Born 1928 & 1922

Shepherd & Gamekeeper

Kilruddery, Bray, County Wicklow

Standing by the sheep-sheds of the north Wicklow farmyard where he has worked for most of his life, 'Red Tom' has entertained a lot of people with his ranting in the course of his eighty-four years. His mouth is on standby at all times, ready to break into a sardonic laugh or a merry curse or an essay of unprintable opinions. The mischievous smile that he sports when he is finished provides the perfect antidote to his wrath.

Today, the subjects of Red Tom's ranting are: (a) the government; (b) modern sheep-breeding techniques; and (c) the more target-specific notion of two young lads trying to cajole him into posing for a book. 'Vanishing Ireland?' he queries. 'Well, my lad's vanishing and I'm getting smaller all right. Next week it'll be gone. Sure they'll save a fortune on my coffin.'

Tom was the sixth of nine children. 'There was no television in them years,' he explains. His father had a small farm near Bray Head. Tom was a young boy when he helped his first ewe give birth to a lamb. He has been a shepherd and farmhand all his life, principally for the Kilruddery estate.

But it could all have been very different. In 1939, young Tom and his sister received an invitation from their mother's brother, David Radcliffe, to go and live with him on his sheep farm in Australia. 'He had 20,000 acres,' says Tom. 'But he had no family so he wanted somebody to take it on.' Tom's mother had sent Mr Radcliffe a photograph of the two children 'in our confirmation rig and he took a liking to us even though he had more nephews than what we were'. The chosen heirs were all set to travel to Australia in 1938 when their parents called the trip off. 'We can't let you go,' they said sadly, 'or we'll never see you again.' And then the war broke out and the deal was off. But Tom was secretly delighted. He remains convinced that if he had gone out to Australia, the Japanese would have captured him.

Tom has never drunk or gambled. 'My brother lived to be ninety-four. And you could say he built the lounge in Lenehan's up above in Bray with all the money he spent on the drink.' Tom's main vice was smoking. 'I'm only after giving up inside the last forty years.' At his peak, he got through a hundred

Sweet Afton a day. 'I'd get them for nothing,' he says. 'I was working for the Passionates that owns Mount Argus. There was one lad called Father Michael and, be janey mac, every time he saw me going by, he'd say, "Here, hold on," and throw me three boxes with twenty packs in each.'

Tom never married. 'I hadn't got time with the scrambling.' In his twenties, Tom went everywhere on a BSA motorbike. 'We took to the old laneways, every which one we could find, and we'd see what was going on up there.' One opportunity to secure a bride came a cropper when he crashed his bike into Bray Town Hall, while 'coming home one night at eleven o'clock, my little girlfriend on my back'. There 'wasn't a scratch on her' but she moved on anyhow.

Red Tom has known Henry Chapman a long time. That said, its only been twenty years since Henry sold his forty-eight-acre farm and took up work as the Kilruddery gamekeeper. As chance would have it, Henry already had several decades of experience in the feeding habits and flight patterns of the pheasant. His father had been a keen shot and bred horses for show-jumping. Henry has an inkling that his forbears were well-to-do folk. Perhaps he is a kinsman of Sir Thomas Chapman of County Meath, who was himself the father to Lawrence of Arabia.

Henry was fifty years old when he took a wife but, content as he is, he is not sure he could recommend becoming a father so late in life – the age gap between him and his daughters has been a complication at times.

At length, the two men head on. Henry makes his way up the Sugar Loaf to look on the pheasants; he will stay there until after dark. With his Madeira felt hat tucked over his ears, Tom is headed for home, to the new house with the new bathroom in it. For all the banter between them, Henry has great respect for Tom after the latter single-handedly re-roofed old Mrs Chapman's house while Henry was away. 'But life was like that in the old times,' says Tom. 'One time you'd whistle and a lad'd hop in over a ditch to help you. Now nobody will do nothing for nothing.'

JOHN SHANNON

1922–2005

Cattle Farmer

Ennistymon, County Clare

When we present Mary Looney with the photograph James took of her late father in 2004, she covers her face with her hands and starts to weep. 'He would be so proud of that photograph,' she says at length. 'He was always dressed up. He said it didn't matter how you were so long as you had a clean shirt, collar and tie.' By good chance, John did actually see the photograph before he died in September 2005. His father had been one of the many small dry-stock mountain farmers living in West Clare. He had five children in quick succession before he passed away suddenly in his late twenties. His twin daughters died soon after and the surviving children were raised by their tireless mother until John was old enough to take over the farm. 'Years ago everyone was very, very poor,' explains Mary. 'They worked hard during the week and congregated in Ennistymon to share the banter at weekends.'

John's son, also John, now runs the farm while his daughter Mary works in T.J. O'Mahoney's Drapers. 'He was a great old worker,' she says, 'and a great one for telling stories. The next generation coming up, we know nothing. All the information from them times will be gone. When you're young, you don't really listen. And by the time you get interested, they're all gone.'

JOS DONNELLY

Born 1919

Farmer

Ballymac, Kinnitty, County Offaly

Our journey has taken us deep into the Slieve Bloom Mountains, once the stronghold of the O'Carroll chieftains and, until recent times, home to hundreds of small-holding hill families. We can still hear the haunting words of Jack Lowry, the blacksmith from Mountrath. 'Oh God there was hundreds of houses up there years ago. The land wasn't good but people lived up there.' Since then, much of the hitherto barren mountain terrain has been acquired by Coilte, the Irish Forestry Board, and planted with conifers.

Joseph 'Jos' Donnelly's crumbling farmstead lies on a plateau of fertile meadows near the Tulla Gap. He inherited the farm when he was twenty and, sixty-five years later, he is still 'feeding calves, pulling buckets around, all that kind of craic', always accompanied by his trusty dog Floss.

'Jos was an awful strong man in his time,' says his old friend and hurling colleague Paddy Lowry. 'He was one of the best friends you could ever have. If you had him on your team, you had all the back up you needed.'

The two men met when they started school in Kinnitty in 1925. Together they learned respect the hard way. 'By God with the hoor of a teacher we had you wouldn't become much of a mischief maker,' says Jos. 'He was a fierce disciplinarian. He would strap you as soon as look at you. But I used to hear them saying they were tougher still in the times before that. It's only in recent times that they've backed off, since the war. I think they were too severe. You got so frightened, you couldn't think. I wasn't ever able to learn much from the age of fifteen or sixteen. The brain was too slow to develop. I meet young ones from the present generation aged three and four, my grandchildren, and they know more than we did at seven and eight! There's no question about that. Maybe it's better teaching. Or better relations with the teachers. And even at home they have a better time. In my time, you might be strapped into a playpen for the day while your mother and father went off to work. It was a completely different world.'

CON RIORDAN

Born 1912

Farmer

Glenbeigh, County Kerry

Con Riordan's home lies in the lush valley of Glenbeigh and, like many Kerry farmers, he has lived here all his life. When we first arrive, his first thoughts were whether or not to don a jacket in the presence of strangers. He's a gentleman of the old school. In his youth, the cottage was thatched but it was given a slate roof a few years ago by a thoughtful nephew. The same nephew looks after the whole Riordan farm now, doing what Con spent most of his ninety-four years doing – 'mowing the fields, planting potatoes, cutting turf, looking after the cattle and sheep'.

The mechanisation of turf came too late for Con. 'Every sod I ever turned was turned with a spade. And when you're gone past ninety years, you've turned a few sods in your time.'

He was one of five children. Their mother died when they were young and their father raised them with assistance from his wife's family. Con's only brother went to work in the coalmines of England but was killed when a pit collapsed upon him. 'The sisters are all gone now too.'

Con is philosophical but restless. 'I can't do a lot of work at my age. When you've nothing to do, you can feel the day. But sure, we still have plenty of time.'

JOHNNY & PADDY WALSH

Born 1932 & 1928

Forester & Farmer

Derrinlaur, County Tipperary

'You see, a tractor could do the work of eight men,' says Paddy Walsh. 'So of course that changed every-thing.' Not that Paddy minded. In the early days, when he first started on the farm at Gurteen le Poer, he might be out ploughing all day with 'nothing to hold only the reins driving the horse'. Over rough terrain on a warm day, with sweaty trousers rubbing constantly against the skin, that could get pretty sore after a while. 'I saw men who could barely walk for a week after,' he shivers, remembering.

Paddy was raised on a farmstead in Derinlaur, a small village pitched on a hill above the River Suir. Derinlaur's history stretches back to a thirteenth-century Norman castle which featured strongly in the Desmond Rebellion against Queen Elizabeth I. Today, not many people have heard of the place – mainly because it doesn't exist anymore. It was effectively abandoned during the 1950s when most of its thatched cottages were knocked and ploughed under. The castle survived but the old village now consists of a few stubborn stonewalls and the occasional banjaxed cartwheel or twisted sheet of corrugated iron.

Amidst such sombre circumstances, it is surprising to find a farmstead where a solitary chimney pot still puffs with a degree of enthusiasm. This is the home of Paddy's bachelor brothers, Johnny and Jimmy. Indeed, this is where all seven of the Walsh siblings were born and raised. Paddy was the firstborn, a bouncing boy who came to life in 1928. Over the next seven years, he was joined by five brothers and a sister before his mother suddenly dropped dead not long after her thirty-third birthday.

Although their mother died young, Paddy says their childhood was a happy one. The boys chased barn owls and hid in the massive fireplace of the old Norman banqueting hall. Their father was a cheerful soul, an old forester who drank a bottle of Guinness with dinner every evening. Sometimes, he would give his sons a quick shot when no one was looking. He kept sucklers, chickens and horses and grew a garden of carrots, potatoes and parsnips. Once or twice a year, he would host mass at the farmstead with the congregation seated on long benches.

Music was another strong feature in those years. Every St Stephen's Day, there would be a great gather-ing for the annual Wren. 'Oh cripes,' chuckles Paddy, 'they'd be galloping about in masks and all dressed up, knocking on doors and dancing around. They'd dance from Kilsheelan to Kilcash and back again.'

In 1943, fourteen-year-old Paddy started work on Count de la Poer's farm at Gurteen just outside Kilsheelan. 'The steward was a man by name of Cummins. He knew my father and asked would I go down and look after the countess' horses. So my first job was exercising horses, riding them up and down the avenue.' At the time, the de la Poer's workforce consisted of thirty people – including fourteen farm labourers, five gardeners, four housemaids, a butler and a gamekeeper. The latter was a wonderful whiskery old Victorian gent from Wicklow, an expert in hatching pheasant chicks. He had them trained to come to his whistle 'but when the shoot came on he'd make them all wild again'.

When not exercising horses, Paddy helped the other lads on the farm, ploughing, cutting, stacking, threshing, milking and such like. He grimaces at the memory of 'sitting under a cow on a warm evening with all the sweat dripping … if the cow had tough tits, you could be there for an age'. Sometimes, he would be obliged to 'milk in the dark'. However, in the absence of electric lighting, Paddy reckons people's visual senses were sharper then and he could fearlessly 'cycle up and down the avenue in the pitch dark'.

Paddy stayed at Gurteen le Poer for over fifty years, retiring in 1994. The Royal Dublin Society had awarded him a special service medal in 1991.

On 2 June 2005, he and his wife Kathleen celebrated their Golden Wedding Anniversary with a party that drew 'substantial crowds' from both sides of the Suir. The couple now live in the village of Kilsheelan with their dog Beckham. They have two children and three grandchildren.

Paddy's younger brother Johnny also started work at the age of fourteen. 'I was in forestry all my life,' he says, stoking the fire in the family cottage where he lives. 'Cutting timber, planting trees, shovelling manure. I gave a lot of time cutting timber with a chain saw.' He points at a scar on his head and says 'that was a close call'. Jimmy believes that the forester's life has become much easier in recent decades but he is not convinced that his successors have a sufficient grasp of the need for conservation. 'When I started, it was all cross cuts and handsaws. It took a long time to get anywhere – months. Then we'd have to haul the wood out with horses – it was slavery really. Now machines drive in and can cut up to a hundred tons a day and they can do it without thinking. And that is the trouble with it. They just do it without thinking.'

PADDY FAGIN

Born 1924

Forester & Farmer

Enfield, County Meath

The road beside us is forever busy with the comings and goings of brave, new Ireland. As I walk with Paddy, a lorry pulls in to his gateway and comes to a halt. The driver, a friend, works with the company charged with quarrying rock for a nearby relief road. Paddy winks at me and tells the newcomer I'm here on behalf of the Revenue Commission. He says I am making some 'preliminary investigations into allegations of misconduct' by this very company. Tense moments tick tock by before Paddy roars with laughter. 'F-A-G-I-N,' he says, 'like the auld lad in *Oliver Twist*.'

He was the fourth of eight children born to a farming couple in Granard, County Longford. His childhood sounds like it was difficult. 'I don't know how we survived but we did. The Lord helped us and pushed us along. There were others who died young.' He does not delve further into the subject and I do not press.

He left school at sixteen to seek his fortune and found employment with the forestry department. 'There was no scarcity of work,' he says of Ireland in the 1940s, 'so long as you were inclined to work. There was plenty to be done. Money was scarce but it was out there. And if you got it, you'd survive. No problem. You would survive.'

Paddy relocated to County Meath shortly after the war. 'I moved to make myself a happier man,' he says, 'but whether it worked out well, I still don't know. I just carried on working.' He now lives with his wife, Mary, in a small pebbledashed cottage by the side of a road near Enfield, County Meath. Their children have grown up and moved on.

'I'm just ticking over,' says the eighty-two-year-old forester, while pouring several litres of petrol from a billy-can directly into a chain saw without spilling a drop. 'And once you keep ticking, you're not too bad.' The chain saw is soon put to use on a sturdy oak Paddy had dragged over from a neighbour's farm with his Nuttfield 66 the day before.

When not collecting timber, Paddy collected things. 'Any old things.' Standing all by itself is a handsome white door that leads to nowhere at all. Beside it is a clapped out Renault that doubles up as a tool box. Instead of a bonnet, an old blue Datsun offers a miscellany of scythes. Elsewhere there are grubbers, ploughs and turnip sowers. Plump red hens occasionally cluck into view. Paddy shakes his head at the sight of them. He confesses that he's never really been fond of chickens any other way than on his plate.

In his childhood, he lived on a diet of cabbages, potatoes, turnips and bacon. Sometimes there might be a lettuce, an onion or some scallions. 'They were all the go that time,' he chuckles. 'You had to grow them all yourself because you couldn't buy them. You can buy anything now so long as you've got money. If you haven't money, you'll buy feck all. It's as simple as that.'

JOHN MURPHY

Born 1925

Farmer & Gardener

Waterville, County Kerry

John's home on Kerry's Iveragh Peninsula had been in the Murphy family for four generations when he sold it to a German in 1971. He and his wife then moved into the town of Waterville, where they still live today.

John's father was one of the principal postmen on the peninsula, delivering mail on foot to households all over a sixteen-mile radius from Caherdaniel to Castlecove. His mother came from a farmstead near Sneem – she was practically the only member of her family not to emigrate to America.

As a boy in the 1930s, John went to the national school in Waterville. 'I think there are only two or three of us living now from that time,' he says. Most of his school contemporaries went overseas. Only 'the odd one came back' and several seem to have met with unhappy fates. 'The outside world didn't agree with them. There was a lot of bloody accidents and things.'

John was a little over twenty when he joined the ranks of the exiles and made his way to England. He found work at the sugar factory outside Ipswich. The pay from the sugar factory was not enough, so he made some 'extra money' looking after people's gardens in the evening. 'Christ there wasn't a worry in the world then! I'd have two dinners a day – one with a lady I worked for and another with my landlady.'

'The next thing, I was shoved into the middle of looking after flowers for the dead fellows,' is how John introduces his subsequent career maintaining a cemetery in Ipswich. 'A cemetery isn't just for burying fellows,' he explains. 'There's a lot of other stuff to be done too.' Working in such an environment gave him a stoic view on life. 'The man who made time, made a lot of it,' he says, tapping his thigh. 'But if you go too fast, you may never make it at all.'

When John returned to Ireland in the 1950s, his experience in gardening stood him in good stead. Until his retirement in the late 1980s, he worked on the 320-acre national park of Derrynane House, once home to Daniel O'Connell. Among the other men working on the estate in John's early days was a former prisoner and aspiring poet, Brendan Behan. 'He was living in digs in the village with his father's brother. An ordinary working man like the rest of us.'

He may have been a gardener, but John has always had an eye on cattle, holding a lush paddock to the rear of his house for grazing. When cattle prices fell, his policy was to promptly make his way 'up the road' and make an offer to any farmer who'd hear him out. 'Ah yeah', he chuckles, 'that was the trick all right.'

He is a generous, open-minded soul. Until recently, he left his paddock open in case his neighbours were passing and wanted 'to put a beast out back for a while'. He is a regular attendant at Sunday mass but has no interest in parliamentary affairs. 'Feck politics, amen,' he says. His particular gripe is against the 'rules and all kinds of feckology that came in about showers and water and things' when he and his wife tried to set up a small caravan park in the 1980s. 'I'd have built houses instead but they wouldn't allow it – and now there's houses all over the place, God bless us!'

MICK KENNEALLY

Born 1939

Potato and Cattle Farmer

Cloonanaha, County Clare

In 1954, the American photographer Dorothea Lange (1895-1965) arrived in west Clare and began to click her shutter. The exquisite images she captured were republished in *Dorothea Lange's Ireland* (1998) with an editorial by Gerry Mullins. Among the subjects in this remarkable collection was a young farmer by name of Mick Kenneally.

This lovely warm man continues to live at the same hillside farm where he was photographed all those years ago, though he and his wife, Bridie, have built a new house. The new build was prompted by the old house being destroyed in an accidental fire in the winter of 1999.

The land between Inagh and Miltown Malbay is a barren, sparse terrain of wet, wet bogs, rickety cottages, glum trees and forsaken grassland. Mick's farm occupies sixty acres along the eastern brow of Mount Callan. The eldest of six children, Mick is the seventh successive Michael Keneally to farm this land. Like his forbears, his day-to-day life principally revolves around donkeys, turf and potatoes. He grew up eating potato cakes cooked by his mother Nora Griffin, another of Dorothea Lange's sitters. 'We used to sow a lot of spuds on the flat land down below. For ourselves and the pigs. But we have no pigs now – and we can get the spuds from the grocer!' He delivers this last line with a hearty, ironic cackle. After centuries of back-breaking work to grow a decent crop of potatoes, one can now pop down to the supermarket and get a bag that's probably been flown in from Poland. In recent years, he has kept the show simple and farms a small herd of dairy cattle.

'It was tough going in those days,' he says of the 1950s and 1960s. 'You'd get up around seven o'clock and keep going until six in the evening. You'd be off cutting turf for the winter. All cut by hand. You wouldn't be kicking inside the bed after a day like that!' Mechanised turf-cutting made life easier but Mick insists the 'the turf you cut with the saw is still a lot better'. As such, he still goes out to cut his own turf by hand. It takes the month of June to dry – or four good weeks of sunshine. He points out the bog where he goes and a nearby ridge along which 'an ass and basket' used to carry the turf. 'Before the tractor it was all donkey work,' he says. 'I used to bring them to town and every place. But there's feck all donkeys around now.'

The local community would gather every Sunday for mass at the church of Cloonanaha. At its peak in the 1950s, the church was so busy that there might be up to a hundred celebrants standing outside. Bridie says the principal attraction was the gossip. 'They'd all meet after mass and stand around chatting for hours. That's gone now. Then everyone got motor cars and they drove away afters. Back then it was all walking. There was maybe the odd bicycle or a few asses and carts. But everyone else walked. You'd wear a white shawl, to keep off the cold.'

Mick met Bridie Corry at the nearby school in Letterkenny Cross just after the war. She was a blonde and he a fiery redhead. 'We were in the same class,' says Mick. 'She used to do the sums for me.' Bridie was a farmer's daughter from across the mountain, the fourth of five girls with two brothers to boot. Her childhood sounds enchanting, dancing around turf fires and 'riding donkeys along the tops of the hills'. The couple married in 1959, went to Dublin on their honeymoon and subsequently raised three sons of their own.

Mick seriously doubts there's much future for the area. 'There's no one around who would want to farm here.' He points to a nearby hill where seven houses were levelled to make way for a woodland plantation in the early 1990s. On another hill to the west, all five houses have been abandoned. 'I'm telling you, it's near wiped out now,' he repeats. 'All the houses are closed down. And all the farmers are buried, dead and gone. When we are dead and buried, it'll all be gone.'

In spite of all of this, Mick manages to retain a humorous, optimistic outlook. Indeed, he concedes that he can't be the first Mick Kenneally to feel that the end was nigh for the rural community of Cloonanaha. Perhaps, he proposes, if they can get the valley connected to wireless broadband, they might attract some new blood.

ATTY DOWLING

1916–2005

Farm Labourer

Tobinstown Cross, County Carlow

Atty would not be drawn into a discussion about his extraordinary tea towel collection – he just stoked the turf fire and changed subject. Now that he is dead and gone, the world will never know his reasons. It is an Arthurian mystery in itself.

Atty Dowling was a lovely man. He lived in a white-washed cottage near the Tobinstown Cross in County Carlow. It was the same house where he was born on 9 November 1916. 'Arthur' was his given name and he was the youngest in a family of three boys and two girls.

His father, Joe, was 'a gentleman, very proper and dainty, always dressed to the nines'. Joe worked in the dairy of Lord Rathdonnell's estate at nearby Lisnavagh. 'It was the heart and soul of him,' Atty said. 'He'd get up in the morning, take a sup of tea, light the pipe and get on to work.' His job was to milk the cows by hand, morning and evening, and deliver the milk to 'the Big House up above'. To carry the milk around, Joe would strap his arms to a wooden beam with weighty churns at either end. The other lads on the farm called him 'The Crucifix'.

In 1919, the deadly Spanish Flu called by Tobinstown Cross and took Atty's mother, leaving Joe and a maiden aunt to raise the children.

'We were five brats,' concedes Atty. My father used to say, "How in the name of God is it everyone else could rare natural childer but my childer are like wildies?"'

By day, the young Dowlings would charge around the house, pretending to be Jesse James or Buffalo Bill, shooting each other from behind the settle bed. If they were still acting the maggot when Joe got home, the exhausted milkman would take off his brass buckle belt and 'lap it around' for a while. 'We'd think he was going to split our skull and we'd be pure terrified – but of course it'd always be the wall he'd hit.' Joe would then calm his riotous brood by sitting them on cushions around the fire and teaching them songs.

In 1932, sixteen-year-old Atty secured a job looking after the shorthorn cattle at Lisnavagh. Before long, he was teaching frisky bullocks how to walk prettily up and down the farm avenue in preparation for the Dublin Spring Show. 'I'd have sooner taken my chances with a court martial but that was the job I got and so I stuck to it.' And he remained at Lisnavagh, on and off, for the next fifty years.

He was a great thinker, a mighty talker, a wholesome vegetarian, a modest drinker. He never married and lived alone, with two cats outside to take care of the rats. He took a keen, if anxious, interest in current affairs and his knowledge of Second World War military campaigns was striking. The last time I met Atty, he poured two large whiskeys and told me his organs were failing. He accepted it as 'natural enough, thanks be to God' and swiftly moved on to the next topic of conversation.

Atty's house is gone now, rearranged, extended, converted. And so too is his immaculate kitchen. The solid fuel Raeburn range, orange kettle ever bubbling on its top. The fridge, stacked with cans of baked beans and processed peas. The box of Daz. The trilby. A copy of the Proclamation of Independence, unfurled from the GPO in the year of his birth, hung between Jesus and Pope John Paul II. On another wall hung the Red Cross certificate he was awarded in 1943 and a blurry photograph of himself as a young man, long of face, bright of eye.

He never had much truck with religious differences. 'That didn't come into anything at all,' he said. 'Protestant and Catholic, we lived as a peaceful community and I hope to God that'll always prevail. There's no use living in the past. We have to try and live in the future and forget whatever petty differences there was among any of us.' But the decline of the Catholic Church certainly upset him. 'It's gone a queer time,' he said. 'And it's leaving us all in doubt because all the great things we learned … we're inclined to think that they were wrong now.'

Nonetheless, Atty forecast a world where 'everyone will practise their own religion and forgive everyone else for whatever their orientation or colour'. The first black man he ever met said to him, 'I hope you don't mind the colour of my skin.' 'I don't care what colour anyone is!' protested Atty, shocked. To me, years later, he confided, 'I have an opinion we're all negroes; it's the climate has our skin the way it is.'

Atty worried that times had gone 'nearly too good'. 'People get everything so handy! In my young day, no one could fall out with anyone because you didn't know the minute or the hour or the day you might have to turn to that person. But now, every one is gone independent, even the poor people, us poor people, and we hardly know who lives next door.'

He says everything went different with 'the Machine Age'. With machinery, came change. 'But,' he countered, 'surely to God nobody will go through the hardship the old people went through. O, God, it was a hard life. Everything – the hardest of work – was done with the hands. But it was a grand life. And whatever the hell way it was, people was somehow happier and more contented.'

Atty Dowling passed away in March 2005.

PADDY LOWRY

Born 1919

Farmer

Forelacka, Kinnitty, County Offaly

He is just getting out of his white Fiesta when we arrive. He gives an uncertain look and wonders what he can do for us. We explain that his friend Paddy Heaney had sent us on down. His cheeks get a little ruddier and he smiles endearingly. His dog is barking incessantly, a big bouncy creature called Darky – 'and other names besides, but come on into the house anyhow'. The house in question is a white-washed cottage where he lives alone. It dates back to the 1830s and was built for his mother's family, the Ryans, who came up from Roscrea.

Paddy is a farmer, descended from farmers. He has cattle and sheep on the hills. In the nineteenth century, his land belonged to the Turpin family who 'weren't the worst but whose agents were devils'. He points to a stretch of land from which, one day in 1844, a man called John Ashton evicted 126 people from Forelacka for non-payment of rent. Their houses were levelled the following day. Among those evicted was a young man called Patrick Lowry. Paddy later discovered a little more as to his namesake's sad fate. 'He was sent to Philadelphia and his wife and children were sent to New York. They were separated and they never heard tell of each other after.'

Paddy's sense of history comes from being located just off the famous Munster Road over which armies have marched since long before Brian Boru's time. As we sit on wooden chairs by the fire, he pulls out a folder packed with information about the area. He shows us IRA lists and eviction lists and census results and accounts from local hurling matches back to the 1830s. He plucks out a letter written by a priest in 1922 relating to the Troubles. The surrounding area had its share of violence at that time. The nearby castle at Kinnitty was burned down. It was rebuilt in the 1920s and is now an upmarket hotel, hosting weddings throughout the year. The castle's wooded boundaries lie not a mile from Paddy's home.

He has never left Ireland but his mind is broad. He is a religious man, of sorts and goes to church to pray but he won't tolerate too much hyperbole from the hierarchy. 'Some of the biggest hoors that ever was were Catholic – and there were some very decent people who were pagans.' Whatever he makes of the sad eyes of Christ on his kitchen wall, Paddy has a healthy regard for pagans. For instance, he is prepared to consider 'some form of levitation' as a possible explanation for dolmens. His curiosity probably stems from being surrounded by the mountain summits where all the festivals of Lughnasa, Bealtaine and such like took place. Even in his youth, the local people would stick flowers into whitethorn bushes and rowan trees (mountain ash) in ritualistic tribute to the ancients. Paddy suggests people were much cleverer in times past, back when faith was guided by the alignment of the moon and stars, rather than sermons and dictats.

His was a small family, just himself and a sister. He was educated in Kinnitty where he met and befriended Jos Donnelly. 'We went to school together, we fought together and hurled together,' he says. Paddy was a keen hurler in the 1940s although he now complains of a 'bockety knee' on account of all the clatters he took on the shins. He also has an ear for the music and is currently chairman of the local Fleadh Cheol. Among Paddy's collection of goods is a photograph of himself, in peaky hat, and a lovely young lady, side by side on the verdant slopes of a mountain. They look to all intents and purposes like a golden couple from a 1950s Hollywood billboard poster. 'Did you never think of getting married, Paddy?' He shakes his head and feigns shock at the very suggestion.

JOHN CODY

Born 1927

Sheep Farmer

Rahanna, County Carlow

He was a great ladies man in his prime – and still would be given the right circumstances. He has that Hollywood look about him, like the kindly old soul who always ends up having secretly masterminded the whole scam. He wears a stripy cream V-neck, a white-collar shirt done up to the top button, navy blue pants and a pair of brown loafers. He pours us glasses of Bushmills, tops them up with 7UP, prepares a brandy and ginger for himself and sits down with his big, broad grin.

John Cody was born in 1927 and bred on the slopes of Mount Leinster. He was the youngest of seven children born to a Wexford sheep farmer. His father claimed kinship with the American gunslinger and circus guru, Buffalo Bill Cody, whose grandfather came from Wexford.

By the time John came of age, his older brothers and sisters had all fled rural Ireland to seek new lives in Britain and the US. John duly took over his father's land – and the flock of sheep that came with it. Ever since, his life has effectively revolved around maintaining that farm. He became an adept shepherd, earning the respect of his peers as a sheepshearer of great precision. One winter, he single-handedly herded three hundred ewes to safe shelter during a particularly harsh snowstorm. That few of these sheep were his own is a fact they will talk of in Rahanna for years to come.

He lives alone in a small cottage on the slopes of the Blackstairs. Mount Leinster rises in front of his home, a mist-covered rocky green landscape broken by stonewalls, lonely trees and mountain sheep. On the summit of Mount Leinster stands the three hundred foot high television mast first erected by Telefís Éireann in 1961. As a beacon for the Age of Television, the mast swiftly became a focal point for debate.

Many admired it, some were in awe and others were determined to fell the beast. In the spring of 1962, John Cody was appointed night watchman to defend the New Mast against any nocturnal saboteurs. It was a role that sat easily with his shepherding duties.

John recalls standing on the summit of Mount Leinster on clear nights when the moon was full. To the east, he could see across the great black Irish Sea and just make out the mountains of Wales silhouetted against the horizon. Had fate dealt a different hand, he realised, then chances were he would have crossed that sea himself.

JACK MacNAMARA & BOB MULLINS

1923–2005 & Born 1921

Farmer & Shrubber

Kilkishin, County Clare & Garbally, County Tipperary

'Sixty-five years is only like five minutes,' says Bob Mullins of his lifelong visitations to the Ennis market. 'When I started it was all asses and carts. Everyone was selling vegetables and turf. The place was amok with cattle and pigs.' 'There's no livestock anymore,' adds his friend Jack MacNamara, otherwise known as 'Jack Mac'. 'They've all gone into the mart now.'

Ennis has come a long way since 1240 when the King of Thomond established a monastery here for 350 monks and 600 students. Situated on the banks of the River Fergus, the capital of County Clare is now one of the most thriving towns in the west of Ireland.

Bob was the third of seven children born to a farmer near the village of Garbally in the beautiful Glen of Aherlow. Since 1941, he has risen at 4:30 every Saturday morning and made his way across the River Shannon to set up his shrubbery stall at the market in Ennis. No other town benefits from his presence but Ennis. 'I love Clare and the people of Clare,' he says, 'and that is a very fact.'

Bob and his son run a nursery in Garbally although he asserts that its really, 'Mighty God who grows them for me.' Bob is well versed in botanical names. 'That's an *aucuba japonica*,' he announces, tapping a spotted laurel. 'But maybe you'd be more interested in a *Fitzroya cupressoides*?' he enquires, patting a sprightly Cypress tree.

'Jack Mac' ran a small farm at Kilkishin in east Clare. A lifelong Pioneer, he was distinguished by his kindness of heart and his prowess as a dancer. He, too, was a frequent visitor to the Saturday market, although always in the role of customer. He would invariably return home to his family with a bag of cabbages and some shrubs for the garden.

The chaotic presence of livestock came to an end with the opening of the purpose-built 'cattle mart' in 1957. Many local farmers initially boycotted the mart but, inevitably, the mart won the day and, by 1988, one of the mart's best years, nearly 92,000 cattle were sold there. Today, Ennis market is all about home furnishings, fashion accessories, cheap electronics – and shrubberies.

Sadly, Jack Mac had passed away by the time we returned to Ennis to talk to them again. 'That poor man is buried,' said Bob softly. We called in to Jack's daughter Suzie in Kilkishin, a MacNamara stronghold at least since 1580 when the castle belonged to Rory, son of Mahone MacNamara. As a cheerful toddler scampered between her legs, Susie sighed that she had not recorded more of her father's tales – 'the old stories'.

Though he bears a tough no-nonsense aura, Bob Mullins continues to regale with his stories. He has a merry twinkle that has given him an iconic status amongst the citizens of Ennis. Younger woman constantly hail the widower and he responds with suitably curt flirtations.

'When that man passes away we're taking down O'Connell's statue and putting him up instead,' laughs Mickey who sells cabbages at the next door stall. 'They will like feck,' says Bob with the vaguest hint of a smile.

MIKE BURKE

Born 1926
Cattle Farmer
Kilmeena, County Mayo

Mike blames it on the tractor. He should know. He's had one for close on sixty years. Before that he had horses. In the early days, the horses did everything. Take turf for example. When Mike was a young lad, he would accompany a horse and cart down to a bog outside Newport. The man cut and dried the turf. The horse carted it home. 'Two carts of turf would be drawn every day,' says Mike, 'and brought home, ten miles each way or forty miles a day if you like.' It was the same with mowing the fields. 'The whole parish was cut with the horses!' But however fond you might be of horses, they just can't do as much work as a tractor. 'The tractor made work awful easy.' That was the deduction of the farmers of County Mayo when the first tractors arrived after the Second World War. And when 'the hydraulics' came in the 1950s, blacksmiths began to hang up their horseshoes forever.

Mike, a bachelor farmer of eighty years, was the second of three boys and a girl born to a cattle farmer and his wife, a postmaster's daughter from near Ballinrobe. His land runs along a secluded chunk of coastline midway between Westport and Newport, the heaving frothy Atlantic tide on one side, jaunty hedges of yellow gorse on the other. The farm also includes a herd of cattle that resides on the island of Inishbee; Mike personally escorts the herd to and from the mainland by raft twice a year.

Like most farmers, Mike is sceptical about the future of agriculture in the present century. 'In the old days, wages were very low and everyone grew their own corn for their own cattle. But now that's all done away with. It's as cheap to buy everything in Westport than it is to get a man in on a tractor to plough and rotavate and drill and roll. The only reason you'd grow your own is because it tastes better!'

Mike also laments the sense of community which he feels has largely 'gone out of the world'. In his youth, all the young women and men would assemble in the fields after they were cut to put the hay up in ricks. It was a time of great co-operation and much merriment. 'We had to build them in such a way that there was no holes on the side or the water would get in and it'd rot.' He says the advent of the corrugated shed quickly put an end to the communal rick-making. 'Well, you could put the hay in the shed at your leisure then,' he says with glum logic.

MICK GALLAGHER

Born 1932

Farm Labourer

Gleann, Collooney, County Sligo

'The cuckoo comes in April,' says Mick Gallagher matter-of-factly, 'and sings her song in May. In the middle of June, she whistles her tune and, in July, she flies away.' We are standing outside Mick's cottage on the slopes of County Sligo's Ox Mountain. He was heading out to check on his small herd of cattle and collect some firewood. Such pastimes keep him active. It's now over forty years since he and his wife left their former home in the town of Collooney and moved 'up the mountain' with their four small children. Collonney was just a village then but 'inside a couple of years you wouldn't know it at all'. At the age of seventy-four, the retired farm labourer certainly seems more at ease at this altitude than he might be amid the buzzing expansion of Sligo's twenty-first century suburbia.

Mick has known Ox Mountain since his youth when he would visit his uncle, a thatcher, who lived in a small settlement called Gleann. 'Every house had a thatched roof in that time,' recalls Mick. 'And when he wasn't thatching, he was making crill baskets for the donkeys to carry the turf in from the bogs. It was all donkeys at that time. There were droves of them on the mountains.'

Mick is not sure where the Gallagher family came from. 'I heard there was an order in for a load of brogues but it was muddled up and they brought a load of rogues instead.' Green eyes twinkle and he breaks a contagious grin. He was the youngest of seven children. His father worked at the Collooney Mills where Mick himself worked briefly as a teenager. He still trembles with the memory of lumbering around hessian sacks of flour weighing anything up to 200 cwt (224 lbs).

When the mill closed in the 1950s, the nineteen-year-old secured a job on the estate of Donal O'Hara, chief of that clan, who lived in nearby Annaghmore. Mick remained there for forty years, despite frequent advice from his siblings to give up on Sligo and move to England. 'They'd be at me to go over every year – but not a bother,' says Mick, whose few visits to England assured him his decision to stay was the right one. Emigration simply wasn't a prospect he cherished. 'I knew a family, seven sons, all fine men. They went to England and worked hard and died young.'

When he started 'above' at Annaghmore in 1951, the farm had one small Ferguson tractor. Everything else was done by men and beasts. Mick was fond of the work horses, particularly one called Smiler. 'He looked like he was smiling all the time but he'd nip you if he didn't know you.'

They were busy days, harnessing horses in the morning, brushing the muck off them by night. And whether it was making hay, sowing oats or cutting rye grass, progress was slow. In time, the tractor came to replace the horse. 'In the end, I was on a tractor, day in, day out. Ploughing in the winter, big open fields of barley, oats, potatoes and turnips. When you've sat on a tractor in bad weather with no cover on you, you know about it. You'd be pure stiff for the rest of the evening.'

One of Mick's preferred sports as a youngster was catching rabbits. 'Annaghmore was stirring with rabbits once,' he says. 'I was very lively at that time and I would be able to dive and catch them. They were lovely rabbits! Roasted or boiled, there was no meat to touch them. It was the healthiest meat you could get. In the war years, the whole country was buying rabbits. You'd get five shillings for a rabbit then.'

In 1954, the decision was made to control the rabbit population by introducing myxomatosis to Ireland. Within a year, more than 90 per cent of Ireland's rabbits had died from the disease. Although rabbits seem to making a comeback in the countryside today, it is still a notable rarity on either 'dish of the day' or the butcher's slab. 'Don't talk to me about myxomatosis!' says Mick sadly. 'I know all about it. I was ploughing them down. They would get stuck on the grips of the tractor. It was unbelievable. I don't see rabbits in this area anymore. They never came back.'

CHILDREN *of the* MUSIC

MICHAEL 'PATSY' FLANAGAN

Born 1924

Drummer & Farmer

Bartra, Lahinch, County Clare

Michael Flanagan looks down from the seat of his open-top tractor and says, 'That's the story now, boys.' In the past five minutes, the eighty-year-old drummer has given us his verdict on the greatest traditional musicians of the twentieth century – box players, pipers, fiddlers, vocalists, flautists, and all. He reels off their names like a sergeant major listing soldiers who did him proud in a war. His knowledge of their miscellaneous vocations is encyclopaedic.

Michael Flanagan is known locally as 'Michael Patsy' to distinguish him from all the other Michael Flanagans in Lahinch. Born and raised to a small farming family in the south Clare parish of Mullagh, he accepts that his claim to be *the* Michael Flanagan of Lahinch would have limited success. But he is probably *the* Michael Flanagan of Bartra, a small beach running along the coast of Liscannor Bay where surfers roam and gulls soar. This is where the bachelor farmer has lived in a small, white-washed cottage since 1949.

This cottage is a simple homestead of yellow walls, colourful dish towels, a big drumkit and a furry cat called Tibby. 'The cat will manage when the man is away,' says Michael proverbially. 'In a country house you need a cat to keep away the mice. The rats and mice that come off the strand – if you saw the size of them! Black dirty things! Nobody likes rats and the old cat will do that job!'

Michael's musical blood flows on both sides. His father was a kinsman of Bobby Casey; his mother counted Junior Crehan and Liam Óg O'Flynn amongst her relatives.

Michael turned to music in his teens. 'I made a couple of tambourines at first. But I couldn't work them so I found a good snare drum and got up with a jazz band.' An army drum-major stationed in Lahinch taught him the finer points of drumming dexterity.

He gives his drums an impatient clatter, as drummers are wont to do, and complains that he's been 'a bit down' with the weather. Sometimes it's not easy being an aged musician. Over the years, he has donned shirt, collar and tie for the Kilfenora Céilí Band, the Mullagh Fife and Drum Band, the Clonboney Pipe Band and O'Boyle's Famous Accordion Band. For thirty years, he drummed for the Quilty Céilí Band, during which time he put in a cameo appearance with the Healy Brothers. 'I'm at it a long time now,' he says wryly. 'Ten bob for six hours work was very handy to pick up in those times. It was good money.'

As well as drumming, Michael can hold a tune on a tin whistle and does a bit of singing. One evening during his youth, he found himself lilting alongside a toothless old man in a small kitchen with a crowd of old women. 'We lilted for fifteen minutes and they danced a whole Caledonian set!'

In 1977, Michael succeeded Jack McDonnell as the Tulla Céilí Band's drummer. Over thirty years earlier, he had actually stood in for the band's original drummer who had fallen ill on the eve of one of their earliest performances, a céilí in Ennistymon. Michael famously sent his drums to Ennistymon on the West Clare Railway, then cycled up from Mullagh with his snare drums, stand and sticks on his back. A few months after he rejoined the band, the Tulla went on tour to England. In 1982, they went on a four-week tour of the USA. Michael returned to America with the Tulla four times before the band's final tour in 1999. In 1995, he performed with them at Croke Park just before Clare won the All-Ireland hurling final and laid the curse of Biddy Early to rest. However, he found the travelling tedious and the rewards unsatisfactory. It's the hazard of playing in a big band – 'there were ten of us to pay each time'!

'Sometimes you can't tell if its a waltz, a foxtrot, a reel or a jig,' says Michael of modern traditional music. 'They play them all at the same speed.' He also struggles with modernised versions of the old Tulla classics. 'It's natural,' he says philosophically. 'Even if you're only digging a hole with a shovel, and someone comes along to make it bigger or smaller, that'll annoy you.' But for all that, he is a great fan of the younger crowd playing today. He holds his neighbour Quentin Cooper in especially high regard. 'I thought he was just a maker of musical instruments but he's more than that. He is a genius.'

When Michael rolls out the big Tulla drum, his brow becomes suffused with emotion. 'If I got a euro for every picture taken of this drum in England and America, I would be down in Lahinch today on the booze!' Being part of The Tulla was possibly the greatest thing he ever did. With the sixtieth anniversary of the band underway, he is hopeful that someone out there will 'walk down to the Tulla Céilí Band and rise it up boy'!

As such, it his annual duty to carry the Tulla drum to Miltown Malbay for the annual weeklong festival held every July in honour of the great Clare piper Willie Clancy. 'I may be coming on eighty-three, but I have a few more nights to be done yet,' he says, tapping his drum with a stick 'If you don't see this drum, then you may take it they've got someone else!'

PAT GLEESON

1913–2006

Musician & Farmer

Belmont, County Offaly

'Mother of God,' exploded Mr Rigney, 'even if I had the brains of Edison and the energy of Mussolini, I still couldn't teach ye.' The schoolteacher's words still make Pat chuckle eighty years after he left the classroom at High Street, Belmont. 'I met him again many years later,' he recalls, 'in a bar in Shannonbridge and we had a drink together and he wasn't as bad as all that.'

Another of Pat's childhood teachers was Mr H. Powers Love, a fervent musician, who regularly came to the Gleesons' house and taught Pat and his sister the violin. The classical style, F-sharps, B-flats and such like. By the 1930s, the farmer's son was a regular feature at the dance halls of the Shannon estuary, always clad in dapper suits, entertaining the crowds with his violin and his haunting voice. In later years, Pat turned his back on the classical and converted to the traditional fiddle. He found the native Irish style much freer, more infectious, a lot more craic.

'Céilí and old time,' murmurs the ninety-three-year-old, supping on a midday whiskey. We are at his home in the depths of Offaly, outside the village of Belmont, not far from the old pilgrimage site of Clonmacnois. This is where Pat lives with his younger sister, Bridget Ryan, and Bridget's family.

Pat and Bridget are two of six children born to a sheep farmer from the Slieve Bloom Mountains. They were raised in a once splendid Edwardian house near Belmont, originally built for the L'Estrange family. An incurable leak in the roof led to the house being abandoned in the 1950s. Today, the building peers sadly out from boarded up windows and wild ivy clambers up the old ballroom walls. Black holes gape where log fires once roared.

Bridget believes Ireland was a much more contented country when she and Pat were growing up. 'There were great friendships among the people. They were always calling to see each other. If you needed a job done, your friends and neighbours would come and help. It's different now, very different. They were happier days then.'

But the past wasn't always a better time. Pat remembers being stopped by the Black and Tans on his way to school. 'They put their rifles up and aimed at me,' he recalls. 'For a bit of sport! I wouldn't have been six years old. They wouldn't have bothered whether they shot me or not.'

Pat was one of countless thousand farmers from the Midlands who never found a wife. Instead, he found respite from solitude playing music in the company of friends, publicans and turf accountants. 'Worry and you'll die,' he says, 'don't worry and you'll die – so why worry?' It is a philosophy he tried to hold with all his life.

Pat still has a great repertoire of rebel songs. The ones he sings to us are sorrow-hued tributes to Mick Dwyer and the heroes of 1798, to those who perished in the Famine, to the fallen brave of the War of Independence. At times, he is clearly much moved by the words, his voice a barely audible whisper. 'They say about the Irishman, his wars were merry and his songs were sad.'

When he sings, his blue eyes invite those who listen into his past – full of crumbling stonewalls, mud cabins, turf fires, long brown overcoats and grinning soldiers with evil eyes.

Pat Gleeson passed away in June 2006.

DONAL DUFFY

Born 1920

Piper

Ravensdale, County Louth

'I'm eighty-six years young,' he laughs. 'I was born on 24 May. Empire Day. The Union flag was flying high over Belfast! Well, the empire's gone but I'm still here!'

Donal has a wonderful laugh, a softly contagious heart warbler which he has been unleashing ever since he first heard my name. He is funny, positive and intelligent and most eager to share the wisdom of his years. He is well known around Ravensdale for playing the pipes at the annual *Poc Fada na hÉireann* festival up in the Mountains of Mourne behind his home.

At times, though, he is grave. Such as when he recounts the events of a cold morning in 1922 when two armed men approached his father outside his home in Belfast's Duncairn Gardens and put six bullets in him.

'At that time, the pogroms were on,' explains Donal. 'Ethnic cleansing! My father was Catholic and we lived in a Protestant area. These two boys were outside the gate. "Are you Duffy?" "Yeh." Bang, bang, bang, bang, bang, bang. Six bullets. But he didn't fall. He grabbed the gate. My mother heard the shots and she fell down the stairs to get out to him. A wee Protestant girl on the far side of the street went for a doctor and priest. He got two in the chest and three in the stomach and he lost the use of his arm. My mother was only a wee lassie. I was two years old. So that upset the whole apple cart!'

Donal's father survived the attack but was unable to work for several years. The young boy was dispatched to live with his grandmother in Tyrone. 'She thought I was God's gift but really I was a wee rascal!'

Before the shooting, Donal's father had worked as a miller. In 1926, he went back to work at the oat mills in Letterkenny. 'We lived in a place alongside the river called Rosewood. That was the nicest time of my life. Hunting rabbits, swimming and fishing after school. I was very sorry leaving Donegal.'

Donal left school aged sixteen in 1936. He needed a career and milling was not an option. As he says, the arrival of cornflakes put an end to oats. That said, he still eats porridge every morning. 'It keeps you fit,' he insists, adding 'with cereals you'd get as much out of eating the packet.'

His younger brother, Jack, would later look west and move to Newhaven, New York, where he still lives. 'He had a better chance because he was the last of us and stayed at school the full length.'

67

But for Donal, England beckoned. Not least when he was sacked from his job at a foundry in Dundalk when he asked for a pay rise. In the hot summer of 1939, a friend from Donegal got him a short-term job as a bricky in Aldershot. A few months later, Donal discovered the streets of London were covered in something even purer than gold. 'Come January, the snow came and it snowed for six weeks and the snow was at least four feet deep. The county boss gave me a shovel and a brush and said, "I don't mind where you go – just shovel. I went up to a seaside place where they were all colonels and generals, and so on. "Mister, can you clean my path, please?" No problem! Ten shillings and a beer every time!'

By 1941, Donal was working as a metal moulderer at the Ford plant in Dagenham. A good salary put him within reach of a childhood ambition. 'When I was a wee boy my father used to promise me he'd buy me a set of pipes, but he never had the money! So I found my chance now. I saved enough money – 29 guineas – and ordered a set from Cork. Then the post office in London told me they'd arrived and there was £25 duty on them. I could have gone to Cork four or five times and brought them back for nothing!'

Nonetheless, armed with his new pipes, Donal had a hobby. He practised by night, much to the pleasure of his room-mate, Paddy Walton, a half-deaf First World War veteran from Cork. 'He was at the Dardanelle's. He told me the sea was red with blood. He was run through the stomach and left for dead. The reason he lived was the Turkish bayonet wasn't fluted like the European one. So they couldn't finish you off. It was like a needle. The Turkish Red Cross saw he was still alive and put him aside.'

Like many an Irishman in London, Donal longed for home. But he was wary too.

'I met this old man from Galway standing outside The World's End pub singing a wee song, 'God Bless the Ship that Brings Me Back to the Old Emerald Isle'. He was one of two brothers. It's a tough life. Very sad. He was a wino. His brother was dead and so we raised a few pounds and dressed him up in a new suit and sent him back to Galway with the coffin. But a month later, he was back again. He said, "It's forty years since I was in Galway before. Nobody knew me and nobody wanted to know me. I want to be back with people I know." That's the sad part of Ireland.'

By 1943, Donal was back in Ireland, kicking a football about with the lads and playing the pipes to his proud father. In 1962, the forty-two-year-old met and married Norah, a Dundalk girl twelve years his junior. 'I wasn't in a hurry to marry,' he chuckles. But it is quite clear that Norah, who bore him seven children and passed away in 1998, was the dearest thing he ever had. They already have twelve grandchildren and three great-grandchildren.

For over forty years, Donal Duffy has been popping through a hole in an old stonewall and out into a magical riverside glade of stately beech, honeysuckle, glacial boulders and rushing waters. In part, this habit stems from his keen paternal interest in forestry. He certainly knows his timber, tapping fallen Spanish chestnuts with a carpenter's eye, keeping another eye peeled for grey squirrels. But the real method in Donal's madness becomes apparent when he unveils his pipes and gets down to some serious practice. One wonders what the local bird population makes of it all.

ROBBIE McMAHON

Born 1926

Singer & Farmer

Spancil Hill, Ennis, County Clare

When Robbie McMahon sings 'Spancil Hill', it all falls into place. There have been so many versions of this powerful ballad that it becomes easy to forget who was there first. Spancil Hill is a small crossroads on the road between Ennis and Tulla in east Clare. In 1870, a young man from the neighbourhood called Michael Considine took leave of his childhood sweetheart Mary McNamara and set off for America. It was his intention to earn sufficient money to enable Mary to join him in due course. Tragically, Michael fell mortally ill in California and died in 1873. Before he passed away, he wrote an extraordinary poem, dedicated to Mary, which he posted back to his six-year-old nephew, John, in Spancil Hill. The poem began:

> *Last night as I lay dreaming of the pleasant days gone by,*
> *My mind being bent on rambling, to Erin's Isle I did fly.*
> *I stepped on board a vision and sailed out with a will,*
> *'Till I gladly came to anchor at the Cross of Spancil Hill.*

Fast forward to 1943 and sixteen-year-old Robbie McMahon is enjoying a musical evening with friends. Moira Keehan, the woman of the house, calls him aside and shows him Considine's words. Robbie reads them, clears his throat and then unleashes his unique rendition of the now immortal ballad. Amongst those listening is an old man by name of John Considine, the young boy first sent the words.

The past resurrects itself as we walk around Robbie's farm and he points out the cottage where 'the Taylor Quigley lived', not to mention 'Mack the Ranger's daughter' (aka Mary MacNamara) and the Considines themselves. Back at the house with our bellies full of hot tea and soda bread, we are treated to the spectacle of Robbie belting out all eleven verses of the ballad. The sky outside is black and wet. Robbie's voice is spine-rattlingly hypnotic, like pebbles skittering across the water. As verse after verse sets sail from his lips, the epic, entrancing effect is heightened by the persistent rat-a-tat-tat of his palm on his thigh.

Not a lot goes on in Spancil Hill these days but it's where Robbie has always lived. He is the third youngest of eleven children. His father was a farmer from the Clooney parish outside Ennis. His mother hailed from Crusheen, a village on the Clare–Galway border. Aside from a sister who died young, the family grew up close and happy. Robbie was a passionate hurler and loved the music. 'The whole lot of us could sing,' he says. Robbie suddenly presents us with a startling impression of her high-pitched voice. He was always the mischief maker of the family, ultimately providing him with the title for his album *The Black Sheep*.

There can be little doubting Robbie's legendary status in the world of traditional Irish music. With his eightieth birthday looming, he maintains plenty of sparkle in his eyes for radio stations and billboards to delight in announcing his anticipated presence at festivals throughout the west. The awards and acclamations have been rolling in since 1956, when he won his first All-Ireland title for singing. He recalls the subsequent evening with a hearty laugh – a raucous session of pints in Duggan's and an old man growling, 'Why can't you sing like your father?' He has since won a further sixteen All-Ireland titles for both singing and lilting. 'The Fleadh Down in Ennis', his anthemic song about the 1956 Fleadh Cheol, is nearly as well known as his rendition of 'Spancil Hill'.

During the 1950s, 1960s and 1970s, Robbie spent several months at a time touring dancehalls, theatres and pubs across the British Isles and North America. 'There was a group of about twenty of us that would go around. Musicians and maybe a storyteller or two. I always did the solo.' There is something particularly wonderful when this quiet Clare farmer recounts memories of Montreal, Minnesota, Detroit and New York. His eyes have taken in a good deal in their time.

He revels in his role as guardian to Considine's ballad. 'How many times have I sung it? Well, it must be getting close to ten thousand times?' One senses he's never far from breaking into a lilt. He frequently cracks jokes, some hilarious, a few unprintable. His anecdotes are filled with memories of the greats – Willie Clancy, for whom the Miltown Malbay Festival is named; the Pecker Dunn who sang about 'The Myxomatosis Rabbit'; the concertina player Chris Droney; the Tulla Céilí Band; Willie Keane of Doonbeg and all the rest.

But for all that, he is a bashful, modest soul and he actually blushes when recalling the time in October 2002 when he came home to find his entire community turning out for a weekend of traditional singing in his honour. 'I saw thousands of cars parked everywhere and I wondered what was it all about!'

Robbie is married to Maura and they have four children, two of whom now live in New Zealand. He goes for a walk every day, lilting as he strolls, his dog Macko running ahead, across the land he inherited from his father. Robbie leases the farm out now, but retains a small patch for growing vegetables – carrots, onions, potatoes and parsnips. On occasion, he will venture to the pubs in the county to hear a session and says, 'I suppose I might sing 'Spancil Hill' again – if they ask me.'

MIKE MURPHY

Born 1937

Fiddler & Taxi Driver

Ennistymon, County Clare

Mike Murphy lives in a slim four-storey townhouse beside Keogh's Grocery on Ennistymon's Church Street. It's been a Murphy household since the reign of Queen Victoria which explains the proliferation of family photographs that adorn the walls and mantelpiece. They include a classic portrait of his mother, a beautiful woman from Mullagh, and another of a young man in collar and tie, an uncle who went to America in 1913. 'And that was the last they heard of him,' says Mike. When it came to emigration, Ennistymon was no different to any other town in the west of Ireland. Week after week, its bright and bold would make their way to America or England. 'There was no other choice. I went for a while but I didn't stay too long. Just for a few months. I didn't like it at all.'

Mike's experiences of North America were altogether happier. From 1964, he toured there seven times as fiddler with the Tulla Céilí Band. Each tour lasted four weeks and took in many of the major cities. Chicago was his kind of town. Toronto impressed him too.

Mike was not trained in music. Few of his contemporaries were. He would listen to his father, James, play the fiddle and concertina. At the age of eight, he picked up a mouth organ and shortly afterwards he moved on to the fiddle and accordion. 'It's all done by ear,' he explains. 'In our time, we only had bits and pieces, no money to buy anything. If you broke a string you'd try and tie a knot in it. Them days are gone though. You pay thousands for accordions and concertinas and anything. I paid over €40 for strings for the fiddle the other day.' He still attends a session once every week. 'The young crowd are great,' he says. 'They've got great instruments and everything but they are very talented too.'

Mike's only complaint is that all those decades spent holding his fiddle high have been bad on his bones. Nonetheless, talk of cod liver oil prompts him to play out the rolls and triplets of a cheerfully haunting tune called 'The Rambling Pitchfork'. The title refers to a wandering farm labourer, the agricultural equivalent of a 'hired gun'. As a step-dance, it was one of the legendary Willie Clancy's favourites. Above Mike's head hangs a 1916 advertisement for Pears Soap. To his right, a piano. To his left, a polished oak dining table still reverberating with the echoes of fiddles, flutes and laughter past.

PAT & JOHN PIGGOTT

Born 1931

Accordian Player & Farmers

Glenbeigh, County Kerry

'Come in, come in,' says Pat Piggott, ushering us in to the farm cottage where he lives with his twin brother John. The rain is bucketing down on the valley and even the dogs retreat to shelter once they've given our knees a cursory sniff. 'It's not too often we'd have people up,' he adds, as we take a seat by a fireplace. 'We'd have more in the wintertime.'

The cottage stands in the lush Kerry landscape of Glenbeigh, sheltered by the Seefin Mountains, overlooking the point where the Behy river meets the waters of Dingle Bay. The region is highly esteemed for its folklore – the nearby strand of Rossbeigh was where Oisín and Niamh took to the sea on their white horse to find new life in Tír na nÓg, the land of eternal youth.

John Piggott thinks their home has been in the family for more than 200 years but knows that it is certainly the same cottage where their great-grandparents lived during the Great Famine. The bachelor twins were born in the cottage on a spring morning in 1931, sons to a mountain farmer who died when they were young men. They also had two younger sisters who died young. After their father's death, they continued to live with their mother.

In the twenty-first century, the Piggot twins seem to represent the spirit of an Ireland that sometimes seems entirely fictional. They wear woollen trousers and sturdy work-boots. They are charming, friendly, enthusiastic men, eager to help in any way they can. They produce a plate of biscuits, a pot of tea, glasses of lemonade ('minerals') and a bottle of whiskey. A settle bed, apparently as old as the house, rests in front of a roasting turf fire. A cheerful green hue runs throughout the house – on the windowsills, the doors, the furniture. On one wall is a picture of a handsome but anonymous woman cut from a calendar long years ago. Beside it hangs a newspaper clipping about their friend and neighbour, the artist Pauline Bewick. A television resides discreetly in one corner of the room. 'It's good for the long winter nights,' concedes John, admitting he enjoyed the International Rules series against Australia.

We sit on green chairs and debate the size of Ireland's thirty-two counties and talk of the extraordinary changes that have already befallen rural Ireland in the first years of this century.

The Piggots are farmers. They keep cattle and sheep in a few fields around the house and have a handful of hens and ducks at their farmstead to provide boiled eggs for breakfast. They have always had their own milk, butter and cream. 'We used to have turkeys,' says John, 'and the pig is gone now too.'

Constant billows of smoke have yellowed the whitewash around the fireplace but the air smells vigorous and hearty. The turf came from a stretch of bog behind the cottage. They had cut it the previous spring using the long-handled slan and pike. Pat is sad that such traditional methods for cutting, stacking and drying the peat are fading away. He fears the increased use of farm machinery will ultimately strip Ireland of every resource it has.

Like many Kerry farmers, the twins have a keen sense of music. Pat is highly skilled in playing the melodeon. 'I learned by the air,' he says. 'By listening,' adds John ingenuously, as if that settles it. The music they play invokes memories of crossroad dances, lush green valleys and Atlantic steamers heading far away. As Pat plays and John taps his foot, we drift together into a distant world where unspoken sorrows mingle gently with hissing turf fires and winter rains.

KITTY CROWE

Born 1926

Singer & Community Champion

Ringsend, Dublin 4

Kitty Crowe demurely clears her throat, closes her eyes and begins to sing. 'Because – because you come to me, with naught save love, and hold my hand and lift mine eyes above, a wider world of hope and joy I see.' Her voice is strong, remarkably so for a lady of such advanced years and she can hold the notes. Her hands weave and part at all the right moments too. I don't know how many times she has sung this song. Niall Quinn heard her perform once. That was when he presented her with a special 'academy award' for her contribution to the community spirit of the south Dublin village of Ringsend. On that occasion, she took the opportunity to deliver some JFK prose: 'It's not what you take from your community,' she advised the crowd when the clapping had stopped, 'it's what you can put into it.'

Music was in the blood. Her father was an O'Hare from Newry, County Down, who, as a young man, took on an administrative post with the new Free State Government in Dublin. In time, he met Kitty's mother, an architect's daughter raised beside the River Barrow in Monasterevin, County Kildare. In her youth, the new Mrs O'Hare had played piano and sung songs with Count John McCormack. 'My father loved music too,' recalls Kitty. 'He would never have let us sit there and watch television. You'd have to get your instrument out and play and if you went wrong you had to stop and start over! I played piano accordion. My eldest brother – Frank, God rest him, he died in London – he had a beautiful accordion. Sometimes, we'd play until six o'clock in the morning! We'd hear the roosters going roo-roooooh and think where did all the time go?'

Small wonder that Kitty should take a shine to a piano player. Dave Crowe was a plasterer by trade and an athlete by nature. He ran cross-country through the Phoenix Park with Eamonn Coghlan Senior and the Donore Harriers.

They met at 'a céilí and old time' in Sandymount. A leak in the roof above had sent a shoot of water down her neck. Wee Kitty O'Hare was a curly headed blonde, working in the Swastika Laundry on Shelbourne Road. Her neighbours would say, 'There's a hare running up the street, d'ya see all the rabbits chasing after her.'

Dave heard her shriek and said he'd fix the leak. His accent betrayed that he had been living in

England for some time. Kitty said, 'Oh no, you would have to be a first-class plasterer to fix that. And we don't need anyone from England coming here to do our work.'

Dave held steady and they were married in 1950. That same evening they hosted an all-night party in the front garden of Kitty's parents' home on Margaret Street. The street, she tells me, was named for Padraig Pearse's mother. And that is where they live now.

Kitty says she remembers the house being built when she was a girl. Her head is full of memories of Ringsend in the old days – of the Gasworks when it was for pumping gas, of endless vegetable rows and 'cattle in the field by Shaw's Lane where the Spar is now'. She used to watch cattle coming through the streets. 'And if I heard a boat coming in [to the nearby docks], I'd run up the big side lane and wave to them. And I'd see a handkerchief waving back and I'd think he's after reading my signal! We'd hear the drones all through the night.' By night, the streets smelled of paraffin. 'It was lovely to watch them lighting the lamps. That was the modern light then!'

In the 1950s and 1960s, Kitty and Dave travelled 'all over Ireland' on a tandem bicycle. It broadened their understanding of the country at large. That said, an anonymous tipster counsels me that whenever he saw the Crowes cycling by, Kitty's feet were always up on the handle bar!

Kitty adores Dave, with whom she had six children. 'You cannot get tradesmen like him,' she insists. One of his tasks was to re-erect the lions heads back on the stairwell of the British Embassy in Dublin after the building went on fire. 'Dave done it and you wouldn't think a match had hit them,' says she. Now eighty-eight years old, Dave quenches his sporting thirst by keeping watch on the Premier League – who plays for who, who's scoring the goals and how much they're earning.

Kitty attributes Dave's continuing good health to a daily bowl of porridge. 'All this stuff in packages now, my father used to say to me, "If I had my foot I'd put them as far as Ticnock." Pure porridge was what the old people took. It was great for the bones. Even for a mother to get a baby started it is the very thing.'

'I've all sorts of blood in me!' says Kitty. 'But anyhow, thanks be to God, I have a good temper and I never got myself into an argument. You have to open your mind. There's no need to be arguing and fighting all the time. I'm constantly offering advice to my grandchildren. More so today than ever before. There's so much pressure and anxiety in the world. You can't expect everything to be there with a click of the fingers. You've got to wait and take your time. Everything is not dull. It's what you make of it.

'And be careful – you can walk the street but you never know what's walking behind you. Joseph [her grandson] says, "Don't say that, Nana, you're frightening me." But you have to! Because there's someone out there who might not want you. It's going on all the time. It makes you sick. I often just wonder if I went up with my accordion, would it ease their brains? Would it make people stop and go right?'

CHRIS DRONEY

Born 1925

Concertina Player & Dairy Farmer

Bell Harbour, County Clare

And down from Bell Harbour Chris Droney he came,

He played on a matchbox – I thought 'twas the same,

Till someone said,

'O Robbie, what's that your saying?

Isn't that his own small concertina!'

Robbie McMahon, 'The Fleadh Down in Ennis' (1956)

'So you're antique dealers then?' concludes Chris Droney when we tell him about *Vanishing Ireland*. The nine times All-Ireland Concertina Champion grins kindly above a soft suntan recently aquired whilst he played concertina on a brand new ocean liner in the Caribbean. He was out with the Four Courts Céilí Band, entertaining 1,800 passengers with a two-hour set of jigs and polkas every evening. The liner was ten decks high and weighed 57,000 tons. 'If you walked a deck three times, you walked a mile,' marvels Chris. 'There was tennis courts, basketball courts, céilí dancing, rock and roll, a casino … they even had a billiards table!'

It's a long way from picking potatoes in the pouring rain, which is one of the more regular pastimes Chris endured as a young lad in the 1930s. The Droney family have been in north Clare for several centuries and it was from his grandfather, Michael, that Chris inherited his original farm on the southern shore of Galway Bay at the age of twelve. In time, the passing of his own father, Jim, left him heir to Bell Harbour House, a handsome gable-ended house built in 1796.

The house, where the eighty-one-year-old Pioneer and his wife Margaret now live, overlooks a patchwork of fields crisscrossed by lichen-covered dry-stone walls running down to the sea. When Chris was young, these fields were the bedrock of the local economy. 'We were always out there sowing sugar beet and corn and potatoes. Every one of them was tilled with horses and ploughed. It was hard, hard work.

You can't see one sign of it now. Not one field! It all disappeared in the last twenty years. They went back into cows first but even dairying has gone by the wayside so now they just leave them.'

Chris' remarkable skill as a concertina is partially genetic. His father, uncle and grandfather were all well-known players and he has an inkling that Droney's have been making rhythmic concertina music since the early 1800s. And it should be noted that Chris' son Francis and his grandchildren are also highly adept at the 'matchbox'.

'Concertinas were very plentiful when I was young. They would have them in every house. There'd be no pub sessions at that time. Just calling to the houses.' Bell Harbour House was a popular venue for such gatherings, particularly for the late-nights of the annual Wren Dance. I started playing when I was eight. I'm seventy-three years playing music now! I'm the same category as Paddy Canny and all those lads.'

'I remember my father having a concertina when I was very small going to school in the 1920s. He got one from London that was a better one altogether and they got better and better.' Chris produces his own concertina which he purchased in England in 1960. 'I went to the factory for a whole day to choose it. I was told leaving home that I was under no circumstances to pass £30. I saw this one and it was top of the range. They wanted £64. I said feck it, it's only once in a lifetime and I'll have it. It's done me ever since and it'll do someone else after I've gone.'

His musical career has been a massive success. Aside from his numerous musical honours, he has played in several well-known céilí bands – he's been with the Four Courts since 1987 – and performed on stages from Toronto to Tokyo. This modest concertina can be heard to great effect on his third solo album, *Down from Bell Harbour*, released in early 2006.

Like his forbears, he keeps a small herd of dairy cattle. They inspire him to head out for a walk every day. As a rainbow sprouts from a rain-splashed sky, Chris starts up a simple jig called 'Merrily Kissed the Quaker'. It brings to mind ancient instincts to whelp loudly, shuffle elbows and skip the feet. He plays the last chords directly at his cattle who, sadly, fail to applaud. 'Not a bother on them!' he mutters.

PADDY CANNY

Born 1919

Fiddler & Farmer

Kilcannon, Tulla, County Clare

In the spring of 1946 a young piano player from east Clare called Teresa Tubridy gathered a handful of musicians from her parish and formed the Tulla Céilí Band. A few weeks later, the band took part in a fleadh in Limerick and won the contest hands down. The now-legendary Tulla Céilí Band held together for over fifty-five years before the death of its anchor, P.J. Hayes, in May 2001. Among the many legends who played with them were P.J.'s son, Martin, Willie Clancy, Bobby Casey and Dr Bill Loughnane TD. But since P.J.'s death, there is one man whose name conjures up the true magic of the Tulla. That man is Paddy Canny, a gentle giant of a fiddler, now eighty-seven years old, who lives just outside the village of Tulla.

Paddy was born in Glendree in the autumn of 1919, the youngest of three sons born to a farmer, Pat Canny, and his wife, Catherine MacNamara. Their family home was the gate-lodge to the once extensive Moloney estate. The Moloney family had left the area when their home, Kilcannon House, was burned in the Troubles and its stone 'shovelled under the roads'.

The Irish-speaking Canny household was also a musical one. Paddy's father was a keen traditional fiddler and specialised in teaching children how to play. 'In his time, there was more music around,' says Paddy with his bashful smile. 'A lot of the musicians he knew were of an older generation. He would keep them in the house for the winter. And then there were people who would call in to visit and he would play with him and I would watch. I was able to pick it up that way.'

A close family friend was Pat MacNamara, a blind fiddler, who stayed with the Cannys during the long winter months. The style of fiddling the two Pats and their friends practised during these years was extremely distinctive, at once earnest and graceful. Indeed, there are many who insist that the entire tradition and style of east Clare's fiddling had its origins in the Canny household.

By the time he was a teenager, young Paddy had overcome his innate shyness to start teaching his own contemporaries how to play fiddle. Among his students was P.J. Hayes and, before long, the two men and Martin Nugent of Feakle were playing at barn dances, weddings and céilís across east Clare. 'The dances started in the schools and then moved to the parish halls. There was lots of dancing here and in east Galway. But then they built the pubs and they took over.' Although he still attends the Willie Clancy Summer School every July, Paddy doesn't enjoy pub sessions. He finds them too crowded and noisy. 'In the old days, if you had a session, you'd have a crowd who were genuinely interested and would either listen or dance. Now they all just keep on talking.'

It was not difficult for Theresa Tubridy to track Paddy and P.J. down and invite them on board the Tulla Céilí Band. In the early days, there was much to-ing and fro-ing to Dublin, the whole eight-piece band and all their instruments squeezed into a Morris Minor. 'It was pure slavery,' says Paddy. 'You would play from nine at night until three in the morning and the wages were pitiful.' Paddy became something of a nationwide celebrity when he won the All-Ireland Fiddle Championship in 1953. He was also a frequent guest on Ciarán Mac Mathuna's programme *Job of Journeywork*. In 1956, the Tulla made their first recordings in Dublin for HMV and, in 1957, they won their first All-Ireland Fleadh title. The following year, they made their debut trip to the USA and played Carnegie Hall on the evening of St Patrick's Day.

Paddy didn't like all this travelling. Since his father's death in 1948, he had been concerned for the future of the family farm. 'My brother Micky had emigrated to England and the other one, Jack, was in Australia.' In time, Jack would return to Ireland and help Paddy look after the farm.

But perhaps above all, at the age of forty-one, he had become a married man. His bride, Philomena, was a sister of P.J. Hayes. 'Times were harder then,' says Paddy of his relatively late marriage. 'It took a long time to earn a few bob, to get a house together and all that kind of a craic. You had to have a bit of cash before you could get married.'

Nonetheless, sporadic tours to the USA and Britain continued until 1963. The following year, Paddy left the band and focused instead on raising his two daughters, Rita and Mary, and looking after his dairy cattle. He yielded his place in the Tulla to an upcoming fiddler from Ennistymon by name of Mike Murphy.

Paddy and Philomena worked the farm together until her death in March 2004. 'She was a great person. But we have to keep on. I trust in the great God above. He never lets me down. I have good health apart from my feet. I get around and do what I want and I'm happy. I have people calling in to see me and that keeps me busy too.' His daughters regularly assign him the duty of 'grandchild watch'. And, once again, there is a beautiful bond evolving across the generations of the Canny family as one of his grandsons, whom Paddy taught fiddle, now plays with the Irish Harp Orchestra.

Paddy's last album was released in 1997. He hasn't played much since but, in honour of my own bride, he plays 'The Monaghan Jig'. I close my eyes and, in the darkness, I see the silhouettes of heels kicking, skirts twirling, elbows flapping, feet stomping, smile flashing, embers glowing, then fading away. His bones ache and his swollen feet hurt but Paddy Canny is at one with the soul of Irish music. He has what his wife's nephew, Martin Hayes, might call 'the lonesome touch'.

CHILDREN *of the* HORSE

DOC MORRISSEY

Born 1935

Horseman

Portlaw, County Waterford

As we walk towards his home, Doc Morrissey turns to me with a wicked grin and says, 'There'll never be another Doc.' This turns out to be a catchphrase in the Morrissey household. Over the next hour, I hear it again and again from his five surviving brothers. Doc is not actually a doctor but, as the seventh son of a seventh son, he is universally hailed as a healer from the ancient world.

The Morrisseys originally hailed from Carroll's Cross in the Comeragh Mountains. In September 1935, three months after Doc's birth, Taoiseach Seán Lemass opened a tannery in Portlaw, thus stimulating a thirty-year boom in the Irish leather industry. Tired of the farming life, Mr Morrissey secured a job at the tannery and moved his eight children to Portlaw. Five of the brothers were likewise employed at the tannery while Johnny, the oldest, and Doc, the youngest, found work at Lord Waterford's stables in nearby Curraghmore – Doc worked so closely with Curraghmore that they eventually named a racehorse for him.

Although the tannery closed in 1980, the Morrissey brothers still live in the house their father first acquired. When I entered the house, three of the brothers were drinking tea and watching a black-and-white war movie. They leapt to their feet at the sight of a stranger and insisted I take their seat and partake of a cup and a sandwich. The television remained on. Along the mantelpiece are various photographs – the Pope, JFK and miscellaneous children of Lord Waterford. I listen to the brothers discussing rashes that couldn't be cured, contenders in an upcoming point-to-point and an old man who used to collect racing pigeons. I have rarely seen kinder eyes.

It strikes me as extraordinary that six brothers could live together in the one house without falling out. Johnny, the oldest at eighty, says they never argue. Doc, born on 17 June 1935, is evidently the most troublesome but, as seventy-three-year-old Tommy says, 'The Doctor would be the most adventurous of us all.'

I asked if any of them had ever married. The expressive eyes of the Morrissey brothers suggest that the notion hadn't really occurred to them. 'The sister might have got married,' says the well-read Joe. 'She would certainly have married,' corrects Mickey, a former tanner. 'But she died young,' explains Doc, and for a moment we are all quiet.

FESTUS NEE

Born c. 1934

Pony Whisperer

Cashel, County Galway

Legend has it that when Oliver Cromwell was emptying the prisons of Ireland during his dictatorship, he encountered a large number of men who had no idea what their surnames were. 'Well, we shall name them after body parts then!' concluded the English military dictator. And so was born the tribes of Hand, Foot, Head, and so forth.

Whether or not this is how the forbear of Festus Nee acquired their surname is unknown. Although he is only seventy-two, there is a certain look about Festus to suggest that he was actually alive during the time of Cromwell. He was named Festus for a little known saint tragically beheaded in Tuscany at the order of Emperor Diocletian.

We encountered Festus on a Sunday afternoon as we were driving around the sumptuous Bertraghboy Bay on the southern edge of Connemara. He was walking to Bolgers Drinking Consultants in Cashel. His motives were two-fold. Firstly, he wanted a glass of whiskey to blast the flu that had been plaguing him for the past week. As he put it, 'I was sound a week ago tomorrow and then the following day I had it.' And, secondly, he wanted to raise a glass to a Fine Gael politician who had died that morning.

The second of seven children, he hails from the Irish-speaking village of Corr na Móna where he has lived all his life. He has found the changes in the past decade overwhelming. He spoke of the 'pure hardship' of his younger days, of tragic deaths in murky bogs and endless rainfall. For many years, he worked closely with a herd of Connemara ponies. He remembers 'the hullabaloo' when Charles de Gaulle and his wife came on holiday to nearby Cashel House Hotel.

Festus Nee is a courteous and kind man and he understands the nature of our quest. He stands by a stone wall, sporting a Texan hat given to him 'by an old girlfriend last summer'. He puffs on his pipe and thinks for a while. At length, he scratches his chin and says, 'No, I'd say all the old timers are gone now.'

JACK 'GINGER' POLE

Born 1913

Vet

Nenagh, County Tipperary

Jack Pole is the oldest practising vet in Ireland. His only rival was Hal Lambert, a vet who also managed to play both rugby and cricket for Ireland. Hal is retired now. 'He's living on his money,' laughs Jack, 'but I'm still trying to earn a few quid.' Jack Pole is ninety-three years old.

His understanding of the changing tides of twentieth-century Ireland is incisive. Perhaps it is the simple fact that he was alive for so much of it. Indeed, considering his grandfather, born in 1830, was a teenager during the Great Famine, Jack Pole seems to transcend all chronological barriers. 'One of my grandfather's duties in 1848 was when his father sent him down to Toomyvara with a horse and cart and a load of turnips. He tipped them up in the village square and people came and helped themselves. If you've a hole in your belly, a boiled turnip is probably better than nothing.'

Jack hails from a long line of farmers from the village of Toomyvara in the northern foothills of County Tipperary's Silvermine Mountains. His great-nephew is the seventh generation born on the land. In 1932, he went to veterinary college and, aside from serving with the Canadian Air Force during the Second World War, he has been practising since he graduated in 1936.

One of Jack's earliest memories was of the Spanish Flu epidemic that struck Europe in early 1919 and which killed over 20 million people. 'Our entire house was stricken with flu. I was the youngest but I think I must have got some sort of immunity because I was always running around with hot drinks. We had no antibiotics. Nothing to treat the symptoms. My father carried on anyway. The farm had to go on. Cows had to be milked.'

Milking cows was a family affair. 'My father started off with as many cows as he could milk and then, as the five of us came along, there were a few more. I milked my first cow when I was five years of age. We finished up with twenty-five cows, three or four each. We'd all sit on out stools and milk by hand. We milked them before we went to school and again when we came back. The milk was taken to the creamery in Toomyvarra with a horse and dray cart.'

Meanwhile, the surrounding countryside erupted in a rebellion 'which started in 1916 and went on until the foundation of the state in 1921'. Jack remembers his father giving refuge to four IRA men on the run. Over twenty years later, Jack met two of these fortuitous refugees. They remembered his father's kindness 'like it was yesterday'. But after independence came Civil War and, in Jack's opinion, 'we did far worse things to ourselves than the Black and Tans ever did'. His mother was constantly herding Jack and his siblings back into the house in case a stray bullet caught them. One day, Mrs O'Meara, who ran a hotel in Nenagh, went out to see what all the shooting was about. 'She was a rather buxom lady but either way a stray bullet got her and killed her.'

In time, hostilities ended and the Free State got a more secure footing. 'I heard my father say that in his time practically every house in Nenagh had changed hands. So changes are ongoing! But it is not long since the small farmer, once abundant in this area, disappeared. That has changed the whole structure of rural Ireland.' Their decline began with the Economic War in the 1930s when the British government slapped a tariff on all agricultural produce from Ireland. 'Cattle, sheep, pigs – you couldn't sell them. Top prime bullocks were sold for maybe seven or eight pound a head. Sheep and pigs would be sold for literally shillings. You couldn't sell a calf but you could sell the skin for ten shillings just to survive.'

In the hard times, a small farmer's staunchest ally was his horse. 'I qualified in 1936 and I went to England and practised there until 1947. That was the terrible winter when TB broke out. But even at that time, most of the work here was done by horses. Irish draughts – the foundation of the horses that made Ireland famous. They did everything. They went to church, mass and meeting. They went to the station with a load of coal. They went to the market with the pigs. They were athletic animals, not like the heavy Shires. They suited the country. But then Mr Ferguson brought in the grey tractor and whatever about the father, the son wanted to get the tractor. So the horses had to go.' Jack Pole asserts that there is not a horse working within a fifty-mile radius of Toomvarra today.

'We had no electric light, no television, no motor car. We walked to school, regardless of the weather. We walked the cattle to the fair. And so, of course, the standard of living now is vastly superior to what it was fifty or sixty years ago. Everyone has 4 x 4s, faxes, telephones, all mod cons. Rural Ireland as I knew it has gone. I'm still part of it and I enjoy living in it. But small farmers have gone the same way as small shopkeepers and are disappearing. Land that was bought for maybe £10 an acre now fetches £20,000 an acre. One has to accept that changes are inevitable.

'And probably, materially, these changes are for the better. But in many other ways, we're losers,' says Jack, pointing at the television. 'We went to the neighbours' houses and we chatted and sang songs and played tricks and enjoyed ourselves. Now you hardly know your neighbours. Young people hardly know their neighbours. It's not their fault. If we were the same age, we'd be the same. They're the victim of a way of life. There isn't the same social contact between farmers as there used to be. Nothing unites people like trouble. We shared everything in the country. If you killed a pig, you'd put it in a barrel, pickle it and hang it up. You brought pork to the neighbours and if they killed one, they reciprocated. There was very close contact and co-operation between farmers and neighbours. It's not necessary now.'

Jack's wife Sheila passed away in 2005, and their three sons no longer live in the area. He lives with his hilariously excitable dog Trixie and keeps himself busy by continuing to practise as a vet, keeping a close eye on the progress of his greyhounds and totting up the number of Volkswagens he's had since 1952 when he owned the first Beetle in Nenagh – thirty-eight at the last count.

JOHNNY HUTCHINSON

Born 1931

Horse Coper

Borris, County Carlow

'I remember hanging the reins up and bending down to fix a spur – and I never remember anything more.' Such are the hazards of working with horses. They can be contrary creatures. Johnny was a child when this kick to the head by a renegade horse left him in a coma for five days. 'Every tooth I had went missing,' he grins. 'They never found a trace of one.' His chest was crushed, his skull split, his nose and jaw broken, and his face absorbed twenty-eight stitches. 'Now I'm not saying I was any better looking before!' he laughs.

'Johnny Hutch' has always lived in a world of horses. On the farm in County Waterford where he grew up, people were forever coming and going with horses. His father was a horse coper, which is to say, he kept a lot of horses and most of them were for sale. When Johnny was a young boy, his father's business went belly up. A promising deal with the Swiss army turned sour in the spring of 1939. On top of everything else, Tom Hutchinson suddenly had sixty-five army horses to look after. 'But Daddy was never one to stay down for long,' smiles Johnny. He did not try to sell the horses. In fact, he began to purchase more – and the traps and harnesses to go with them. Then he put the whole lot into stables and declared himself back open for business.

'In my place you never asked questions,' Johnny says. 'He was always gone too quick; there wasn't time to answer them.' At the close of 1939, when the Second World War exploded, petrol was scarce. Before long the Hutchinson horses were doing work for 'every miller, draughter and farmer in the land'. The lost fortunes were quickly recouped, a happy turnaround for a man with ten children.

'My first job,' says Johnny with one eyebrow higher than the other, 'was to walk the hay – walk, walk walk, trample it down, get it good and flat so it could be gathered more easy.' When Old Man Hutch felt the boy was ready to learn the true art of horsemanship, he sent him to school with a White Russian émigré called Colonel Paul Rodzianko. Considered one of the finest horsemen in the world, Rodzianko had been among the first to discover the bodies of the Tsar and his family at Ektainberg in 1917. He was 'a fantastic trainer,' concedes Johnny, 'but he was a pure cruel man, and as likely to put the whip on a boy as he would a pony. If it were now, he'd be locked up for all time.'

In time, like his father before him, Johnny became a familiar figure amongst the hunting set. Under the mastership of the McCalmonts of Mount Juliet, the Kilkenny Hunt offered some of the best hunting – and parties – in Ireland. 'They were great old times. Everyone was wining and dining and loving the old hunt.'

When not hunting, Johnny trained horses for both the show ring and the gallops. Together with his wife, Mary, he still runs a riding school and operates a livery yard. Age has not slowed him. 'I can still enjoy the riding like I did when I was seven,' he insists. But he speaks of the old days with melancholy. 'It was much simpler,' he says, 'when it was all about the craic.'

RORY KILDUFF

Born 1922

Saddler

Ballinasloe, County Galway

'Those stories I told you are true,' says Rory Kilduff, leaning back in his armchair, 'but I could make up a few if you're stuck.' His wife, Maura, plants a tray of biscuits and tea on the table and beckons us help ourselves. In the space of thirty minutes, Rory has already unleashed a dozen yarns relating to the life and times of Ballinasloe, the east Galway town where he has lived for the past eighty-four years. He is absolutely delighted to have the opportunity to recount his memories aloud. Barking a familiar cry about the disinterest of youth – 'the television has made everyone so smart, we're all gone cracked'.

He describes his childhood as 'a comical time'. In summer months, 'a contrary fellow' named Burke drove a horse and water-cart down the streets to keep down the dust. 'We all wore short pants at that time and so we would get rid of our shoes and follow the cart and splash in the water jets.' Burke was unimpressed. 'He would let the whip fly and, if he got you, he'd cut the ear right off of you. "Let the water on the road," he'd say. You'd think we were going to put it in our pocket and bring it home.' There can be little doubt Rory and his pals weren't all sweetness, as he tells a tale of them sneaking up to the bank manager's tennis courts and 'parroting the well-to-do voices' of the players until the bank manager gave chase, but 'sure, we were only eight or nine and he wasn't ever going to catch us'. A while later, the young crew were gawking out the window from Cullen's the Drapers to watch the arrival of electrification in 1929. 'T'was a wonder of the world seeing this light going on.'

His merry bespectacled eyes beam at the memory of the night Old Man Higgins lit an ill-advised fire out the back of Harper's hardware store and nearly burned Ballinasloe to the ground. 'Harper's used to sell guns and gunpowder for all the muzzle loaders out the country,' laughs Rory, who was seven at the time. 'The explosion blew all the windows out of Society Street and every second ceiling fell down.' Higgins was exceedingly fortunate. 'It's a strange thing but gunpowder apparently takes the easy way out and the blast went out over him.'

If Rory has a moral to this story it is that 'the people who had their windows blown out never looked for a penny's compensation'. He says nobody ever sought or expected compensation – not until the motor car began knocking people about. Like his neighbour, poor Margaret Doran, who became the town's first road victim when she was killed by a reversing Buick at the Fair in January 1928. 'She was a miser,' says Rory conspiratorially. 'She made her fortune by selling turf to the poor for a penny a sod. A week after her death, her husband went into a shop on Main Street with 600 sovereign coins and said, "Give me paper for that … this is far too heavy to carry."'

Rory is entitled to cast a dirty look at the motor car because the car and the tractor put paid to the Kilduff's family business as saddlers. The family involvement began in about 1880 when Rory's father, the son of a farmer from Kilbegley, purchased the saddlery from his former employer, Mr Grainey. During the Land Wars of the late 1870s, the older Kilduff assisted Mr Grainey in making a particularly beautiful harness for a local gentleman with buckles and fittings that were silver-plated in Walsall, England. When the gentleman was subsequently assassinated, Grainey wrote to the dead man's brother in England requesting payment. By chance this brother was director of the Walsall silversmith. He wrote to Grainey: 'If you and your countrymen didn't shoot my brother, I'm quite sure you'd have got paid for your harness.' Grainey replied: 'The pity of it was that me and my countrymen didn't shoot you and your brother long ago, and I'd still have me harness.' And that, concludes Rory, 'finished the deal'.

Rory had not intended to become a saddler but his father had a heart attack and he was obliged to plug the gap. Then his younger brother Brendan died of meningitis on his eighteenth birthday and his only sister had married and moved on. 'It was a slow old thing to learn and I didn't know anything much but I was able to cut out the patterns of the saddles and collars.' With the outbreak of the Second World War, 'it got busier and busier and I learned it'. But then 'the tractor came in and [the saddlery business] died'. An old farmer called Paddy Walsh made a concerted effort to stop the rot. 'He went walking up and down outside the Dáil with a placard that read: 'No Tractors in Ireland' … wasn't he fierce daft! Poor Paddy!'

Rory walks us out to the rickety old saddlery yard adjoining his three-storey home on Ballinasloe's Main Street. He shows us the workshop where, in his youth, twelve men worked full-time, making harness straps for driving horses and draft horses, purpose-built for ploughing fields and cutting hay. He shows us the ghostly relics of harnesses, pommels, bridles, nose-bands, gauge knives, collar-irons, silver plate buckles, floppy stirrups and broken mallets. The air is scented with leather. He says there is absolutely no demand for harnesses today – 'save for the Travellers'. As we walk about, Rory relives the days when all the rollers and drums and mallets and hair-machines were clanging and clinking. He says that, as Kilduff's were the only saddlers in Ballinsloe, life was particularly hectic during the annual horse festivals. 'When I'm dead and gone nobody will know what all these things were for!' he chuckles, tapping a classic Harland & Wolff hames collar with his cane.

MICK LAWLOR

1927–2004

Trap Driver

Borris, County Carlow

Mick Lawlor died two days after James photographed him. It was not his intention to die quite so soon, he had invited us back the following week to join him for a tour of his neighbourhood on his pony and trap. His home lay in south County Carlow, close to the village of Borris, with excellent panoramic views of the fertile lands of Kilkenny to the north and the mountains of Wexford to the south. Scattered around the immediate vicinity of his home were various items he had collected along the way – a bathtub, a Belfast sink, a wooden barrel, a milk churn, a pack of loose-knit fence posts and some bails of wire, concrete blocks piled high in six deliberate columns, one forming the shape of a staircase.

His house was a bungalow, the exterior walls resembled a tiled motel bathroom, with a bright-blue double door serving as the principal entrance. The interior consisted of three rooms – one for his kitchen, one for his bedroom and one for his jennet, Pegasus, the driving force behind his trap. Alas, the jennet's room lay empty for his beloved comrade of twenty-seven years had died three weeks earlier.

When he offered to take us out on his pony and trap, he had to scratch his head and think where he might source another pony for the occasion. There was a sad look about him that suggested jaunts around the countryside could never be the same after Pegasus. Some consolation may have come from Sheba, his seven-year-old sheepdog who literally put her hand out to introduce herself when we arrived. Mick also maintained that Sheba could tell the time of day by looking at the clock on his kitchen wall.

BILL BURGESS

Born 1902

Amateur Jockey & Farmer

Tobinstown, County Carlow

On his mantelpiece stands the Centenarian's Coin awarded to him by President McAleese on 23 June 2002, surmounted by the four coins presented on each subsequent birthday. At the age of 104, Bill Burgess presently ranks as the fifth oldest man in Ireland.

He was born in June 1902, a month after the Boer War finally ended. He was ten years old when the *Titanic* sank, fifteen when his brother Rupert was killed in action in Belgium, twenty-seven when Wall Street crashed, thirty-seven when Hitler invaded Poland, sixty-one when JFK was shot, seventy-seven when the Pope visited Ireland, eighty-seven when the Berlin Wall came down and ninety-nine when the Twin Towers collapsed.

His grandfather came to Tobinstown as a tenant farmer in 1852 and built the granite farmstead where Bill now lives with his son Edwin and Edwin's wife, Nora. Bill's father inherited the farm in the 1890s and married a Dublin girl with whom he had ten children.

'I was the fifth boy,' says Bill. 'There were two boys, two girls, then a boy, a girl, another boy, then me and two girls after. If that sounds like a handful,' he says with a contagious grin, 'then the neighbourhood must have been pure chaos. There were thirty-three children between three houses – we were ten, the Ryans had eleven and the Fishers were twelve.'

In March 1909, Bill's father passed away with acute peritonitis. 'The night he died, we were called over to his bedroom to say goodbye. I was six and my younger sister was a year and a half. I remember her crawling up and putting her hands around to say goodbye to him.'

In June 1917, Bill's elder brother Rupert was killed fighting for the Australian army at Messines Ridge in Flanders. And then, in 1919, came the Spanish Flu, a horrendous epidemic that annihilated more than 20 million people. Bill had been sent to school in Dublin the previous September, 'very much against my will'.

'It was the end of October when the schoolmaster came up to me. He was a savage man. He should have been locked up in Mountjoy. He told me a wire has come and asks: "Have you a sister, Vivian?" I say, "No, I've a brother Vivian". Vivian was two years older than me, as hardy a young fellow as you'd meet. "Well," he says, "he's dead." Just like that. If he had hit me between the eyes he couldn't have done more.'

Bill joined up with two of his sisters living in Dublin and went home immediately. 'A man met us with a pony and trap,' he recalls. 'My brother was dead. Another brother and three of my sisters were down with the flu. There was no antibiotic and no whiskey either. There was nothing to be had. No up-to-date medicines. No pick-me-ups. Nothing. Dr Kidd in Tullow recommended we get some whiskey or poitín but even that was hard to find.'

Fortunately, the family recovered strength and, by the mid-1920s, Bill was fast establishing himself as one of the most proficient amateur jockeys in Ireland. 'I was like our Lord at the beginning. I started out on an ass before the war. An ass with no hair and four legs!' He quickly progressed to proper hunters, sturdy beasts with names like Quick March, Lightfoot and Fearless.

In April 1926, Bill mounted a horse owned by his brother Harry – 'very badly wrong of wind' – and rode him to victory over twenty-six jumps in the Farmers & Members Race at the Coolattin Point-to-Point. He would go on to win the same race on five further occasions, as well as numerous other races at meetings throughout Ireland.

'I rode different places for no advantage to myself, only disadvantage. I got no money. You could call it sport if you like – risking your neck on every fence! But you do things at twenty you won't do at thirty, much less at forty.'

He points to a photograph from 1935 of a stocky young lad seemingly flying through the air. 'That was taken at the last double-bank in Coolattin. I was fired head-over-heels over it. The horse was Brown Jack and he ended up dead on one side and I landed on the other with a dislocated ankle. I hopped up as best I could. I got up on another horse and I won the next race.'

On another occasion, he was invited to Kilmallock to participate in a race. 'I got my breakfast here at eight o'clock in the morning and I went the hundred miles with my brother-in-law. That was a long journey. We walked the course and I rode the race and I won a prize for the owner of £25. Afterwards, he gave me great praise and asked would I like a drink? I wasn't a drinker anytime so I said I'd have a grapefruit. It cost the sum of four-pence in the ordinary way. And that's all the thanks I got. I nearly gave up riding after that.'

When he wasn't riding horses, Bill was running the family farm, harvesting wheat and supplying milk to the Lucan Dairies in Dublin. In 1957, he married Dolly but it was to be a dreadfully short marriage. 'Two and a half years later, I was back in church again to bury her.' He was left with a small boy, Edwin.

Bill is an old-school gentleman. He stands up when someone enters a room. He insists on walking them to the door when they leave. He believes that life is a precarious affair and every moment of happiness must be appreciated. 'Isn't it a funny thing,' he remarks, 'that of all the men and women who ever walked this earth, not one of them ever knew what happens afterwards?

'I have no control over it,' he says of his longevity. 'But when I've gone? Well, as the man used to say when we'd meet on a bank in a chase, "Cheerio till the other side!"'

JACK LOWRY

Born 1923

Blacksmith

Deerpark Forge, Mountrath, County Laois

Jack Lowry and his wife Nora live in a neat two-storey building at the foot of the Slieve Bloom Mountains. The house, with a Famine wall nearby, dates to the 1840s and was originally built by the Coote family of Ballyfin for their carpenter and blacksmith.

Jack was the second of five boys. Although the family owned a ten-acre farm, his father – and grandfather – were first and foremost blacksmiths. 'My father was nearly sixty when he married and lived to be ninety-five. The way it was, he shod the horses and the people paying for the horses would do the farm work. It was all more neighbourly like.'

One of Jack's earliest memories is of the Big Snow of 1932. 'The weather them years was different to now, much harder. In the winters, there'd be a terrible lot of snow and frost. Now there's very little snow. When the Big Snow came, I was only nine. It fell on a Thursday night and by Friday morning the windows were all dark. The snow was lying against them. I opened the door and two feet of snow came in on me. I got a powerful knock. I can remember my breath was near going away. There was a storm along with the snow and it blew all the snow so it banked up against the houses. The whole country was level. You'd only see the top of the trees. There were places where there was twenty feet of snow. There was very little food around then. A loaf of bread, some flour, a few eggs. Some were near starving because they couldn't get to their neighbours. People got out and started digging along the road and finally they got into Mountrath the following week and that was the relief. There was never the like of it came since.'

In his teens, Jack was educated at nearby Ballyfin, in what was once the Coote family seat before it was converted into a school by the Patrician Order in the 1920s. He left school at sixteen to follow his father into the blacksmith's profession.

'I was about thirteen years old when I shod my first horse. We'd always be here, repairing farm implements and shoeing horses. In the springtime, it would be all ploughs, harriers and cultivators. Then you went on to mowing machines, blades and that. Then, in summer, binding wheels was a big job. We'd often be at it until three or four o'clock in the morning. But at that time, there were forges everywhere. There'd always be people passing on bicycles or maybe with a horse and cart,' recalls Jack. 'They'd call in for a drink or have a talk or maybe light a pipe. Matches were scarce! They were always talking! My father would work away, just carry on, leave them to it. He'd have to make peace sometimes when they'd get to fighting over politics. Then there'd be all the talk about hurling and football matches. My mother made them all tea. People could be waiting here a long time. There might be three or four horses in front of them, so she'd bring them in for a cup of tea.'

Later on, Jack takes us to his forge where rusty tools remain optimistic of a renaissance in smithery – tongs, mallets, springs, anvils, bellows, grinders. Beside the same old hob his grandfather used a century ago is the basin in which red-hot horseshoes once hissed.

Blacksmiths have been around since the Iron Age but Jack can't see the profession surviving for much longer. It's already become a specialist world where your best hope is to secure contract work with a racehorse trainer, like Jack's son Martin who works with Charlie Swan. 'Everything changed after the war when the tractors came. That's when the farm-horses began to go. By the 1960s, it was nearly all machinery.'

The advent of rural electrification sped on the blacksmith's decline. 'When I began, the work I did was the same as my grandfather. It was heavy work and everything was done with fire and that was the way it was done. But then we got welders and drills and it became much easier. There was terrible work trying to get people to get in the electric. The parish priest had to go around and convince everybody. People were very poor then. I remember asking one fellow, "Are you getting in the electric?" He was coming out of a shop at the time and he had a gallon can of paraffin oil on him. "Oh no, what would make me get electrics?" says he, "Sure that'll do me a fortnight."'

Jack and Nora have two daughters and a son. Nora loves dancing and attends céilés in Nenagh twice a week. Jack says he was never a great one for the dancing and prefers playing cards – Twenty Fives is his personal favourite.

CHILDREN *of the* TRADE

MICK STANTON

Born c.1930

Fruit Seller

Kinvarra, County Galway

Everyone out west has heard of Mick Stanton. He's the market man, the fellow with the hat who sells the fruit and vegetables. And when the market shuts up, he can be found at his favourite bar in Ballindereen. Or is it Vaughans of Kilfenora? At any rate, we found him in Rafferty's Rest of Kilcolgan.

Mick orders me a pint. 'Its tradition,' he states, 'that if you were here longer, then you stand a drink to anyone joining you.' He is a funny mischievous man who takes life easily and makes me laugh.

I still don't know what age he is. Initially, he said he was eighty-two. Then he said he was only codding and he'd be sixty-eight in July. And, finally, he said he'd been doing the market thing for at least sixty-five years. It's the way he is. He talks in riddles. When I ask how big his family is, he replies, 'I have four sisters and everyone of them has a brother.' It takes me a while to figure out that he comes in the middle, sandwiched, as it were, between sisters. Whatever about the year he was born, his place of birth was Kinvarra, a colourful fishing village on the southern shore of Galway Bay.

Everyone knows him wherever he goes. 'I call myself a Clare–Galway man,' he says diplomatically, 'but its true the Clare people do appreciate me.' He is perhaps referring to his recent anointment as 'best dressed man' at the Galway Festival by *The Clare People.* Mick is a married man with four children. I met one of them later who assured me this was true.

He sets up his stall five days a week – primarily in Roundstone, Connemara or Ennistymon, but also on the streets of Galway town. He has been selling apples and oranges all his life. He has a vigorous respect for the mysterious ways of Irish Travellers. When his sister inadvertently ignored the Travelling woman called Biddy Ward, she invited upon herself an unusual curse. 'She had twin girls before the year was out!' he whispers conspiratorially.

'I've met tinkers and tailors and soldiers and sailors,' muses Mick. 'Rich men and poor men and beggars and I never fell out with any of them.' If people are short a few euro, he will let them off. 'That's what I've done forever and I'm not going to change it. Everything evens out in the wash. What you give comes back double.' He knows this is a powerful truth although personally I wonder does this mean I now owe him two pints?

JOHN FLYNN

Born 1943

Thresher

Ballyduff Upper, County Waterford

'I'm Ballyduff baptised, Ballyduff confirmed and Ballyduff married,' says sixty-three-year-old John Flynn, with a nod, a wink and a grin in equally quick succession. He is a big friendly man, much respected by his fellow villagers. As a child, he spent many long hours helping his father thresh and bind corn for farmers along the Blackwater Valley. 'We had a mighty business going at one stage,' he recalls. 'We'd be started with the cutting of the corn on 15 August and we would not finish until the first days of December – and once or twice up to Christmas itself.'

The arrival of combine harvesters in the late 1960s 'pulled the plug on the threshing' – and the dancing that went with it. The Thresher's Dance was one of the highlights of the calendar for the rural community. Covered 'in chaff and oil and cabbage', everyone would set to in the kitchen, dancing jigs and twirling reels, as local musicians played on melodeons and fiddles. 'They'd maybe have a keg of porter or two and they'd go until three o'clock in the morning, nothing more.' His grandfather hosted dances once a week at his home. 'He was a great accordion player and used to play on the stage at Mocollop Cross. My mother was lovely at the waltz.'

Aside from music, John's great passion is for very old tractors. He regularly tours Munster's vintage rallies with a 1947 Allis Chalmers WC, all the way from Wisconsin. From his pocket, he plucks an article about a steam engine that has just re-emerged on the coast of Florida seventy years after it disappeared. He gazes at the photograph with the same reverence Darwin might have bestowed upon the newfound skeleton of a Tyrannosaurus Rex.

He is reorganising his hardware store when we arrive. 'It's hard to get things out,' he explains, 'because one thing is in front of the next.' The building was originally the school but closed in 1979 when a new school opened just outside the village. John says the Ballyduff of his youth was a vibrant place, awash with donkeys and carts coming to and from the creamery. Now, the village struggles to cope with an endless reel of juggernauts, buses and cars pouring over the old bridge across the Blackwater. Where once there were nine grocers in the village, now there are only two.

BOB MURPHY

1909–2002

Gardener

Rathvilly, County Carlow

Bob grabs my hand suddenly and whispers: 'That man there … d'you see him?' I look across the ward at another old man, lying down, itching his back. 'He's armed,' says Bob, his eyes wide. 'With a six chamber pistol.'

I think 'Ah!' and recall Bob's paranoid visions the night he was taken into hospital in Carlow. Dear old Bob. The dapper gent of the mushy-pea suits, the feathered trilbies and the coal-fired greenhouse. It's odd to see him here now, laid up in a hospital bed dressed in pale blue pajamas, convinced he's got a homicidal maniac two beds over. Fair play to the old boy though. Bob liked his drink but he hasn't had a jar in over a week. But now he looks at me and says, 'Maybe I'll live to be a hundred,' and guffaws and we're all grand again.

He did get out one more time before he died. A friend whisked him over to Molloy's, his favourite haunt, for a farewell drink. Eithne Molloy caught a tear rolling down his cheek as he made his way out the door for the last time. 'He knew the end was upon him,' she says. She had known him all her life. Everyone in Rathvilly knew Bob. 'He was an icon,' declares Betty Scott, who lived in the cottage next door to him.

Bob was well known to most drinking establishments in north County Carlow. He was a quiet man but he loved the craic. His tipple was whiskey and 7Up, or a '7½?' as he called it. Betty would hear him being decanted onto his doorstep by a friendly chauffeur at four o'clock of a Sunday morning and not hear another peep from him until Tuesday evening. 'He was in dry dock, you see,' explained Betty.

He was the second youngest of seventeen children born to an assistant gamekeeper at my family's estate outside Rathvilly. Most of Bob's siblings emigrated to England or America in the first three decades of the twentieth century. He never even met some of his older brothers. 'They are all gone now.'

During my childhood, Bob was simply Bob, the funny wee fellow with the cowboy hat who stood in the doorway of his home nodding his head at us when we went to visit Betty. Then, one afternoon, I met him looking befuddled, standing by the road outside his house. He was awaiting the two o'clock bus to Tullow. It was two forty-five. After talking to him for a while, he realised the problem – autumn had begun the day before and his watch was an hour fast. Easy mistake, easily rectified. Bob duly tapped his watch, dismounted the wall and disappeared into his house. I waited uncertainly. He returned, strapping on a new watch. He explained that he had two watches – one came off at summer's end; the other went on for the spring.

I was only in his cottage once. From the outside, it was small, yellow and deceptively quaint. The windowsills and drainpipes were powdery blue and a pretty scarf of pink ran around the base. The interior was another matter. Flailing red strings of peat briquette wraps. Upset primrose pots and chippings of terracotta. A soot-encrusted sofa with springs squiggling north and south. Open pots of blackberry jam with upturned lids looking like nightclub ashtrays. An eruption of loose black-eyed spuds galloping into the next door room. Betty claims that Bob never got ill. 'There's no germs alive that could have survived in his house,' she reasons.

Bob's greenhouse was wonderful. It occupied an old pig-sty to the rear of his house, accessible via a shed full of old furniture and Nellie bikes. The greenhouse was Bob's pride and joy. The soil was freshly raked and weedless; the petals wholesome and bright. Around the perimeter ran a thick pipe connected to a small stove, fed with coal nuggets in the colder months. It was so incredibly pleasant there that I sometimes wondered if that was where Bob actually slept.

Betty adored Bob to bits, but never allowed herself to call him anything other than 'a feckin' torment'. She is still full of anecdotes about the bachelor's persistently 'bauld behaviour', his quick-fire one-liners, his stubborn resistance to doctors and priests, his merry tours of the region's drinking emporiums, and such like. When Father Flood came walking past their house one day, Bob drolly mumbled, 'That's the first time I seen a flood coming uphill.'

When he didn't mumble drolly, he was still impossible to understand. His voice belonged to another generation. From his hospital bed, I deciphered a little about his life and how he advanced via England from raking lawns for 'The O'Byrne' in Kildangan to laying pipes in glasshouses and pitching netting over the roses of my own late grandmother. His favourite flower, he confided, was a blue rambling rose.

On another occasion he told of Kevin Barry, the patriot from Rathvilly executed in 1919, standing up to a bully of a teacher and getting his ears smacked for his impudence. Betty tells me Bob was the second youngest of seventeen children. 'We won't get those people again,' said Betty. 'Bob was the end of an era.'

As chance would have it, Bob's funeral was presided over by Monsignor Deering, a Rathvilly citizen who had moved to Waco, Texas, and came to fame as 'the Pastor with the blaster' during the David Koresh debacle. The monsignor was on a return visit to Ireland and had known Bob in his youth. 'We all gotta go sometime,' he drawled to the gathered mourners. 'And Bob knew his time had come and he opened his arms to the Lord and said, "Take me away, Father." Well, Bob, now that you're up there, why don't you plug in a light for all of us!'

Bob would have loved it.

TOM FRAWLEY

Born 1920

Publican

Lahinch, County Clare

'If priests were allowed to marry, they wouldn't have had half the number of scandals.' When Tom Frawley makes his point, he does not slam his fist on the bar. He says the words with quiet certainty. He has thought the matter through thoroughly and he knows he is correct. Besides which, the bar is his so why would he want to go and bang it?

Tom has been pulling pints in County Clare for seventy-seven years. He watched the first one settle when he was nine years old. The pub in question is named Pat Frawley after his father and occupies a discreet position in the seaside village of Lahinch. It has been operational since 1880 and came into the Frawley family when a great-aunt married the original owner. Tom's mother inherited and ran the pub until her death in 1961 when Tom, her only child, took it on.

Forty-five years later, the octogenarian bachelor keeps a simple bar. It is a place for quiet indulgence and brief philosophy. Although we are told by others that Tom has a fine voice, he claims to be wary of musical sessions getting underway in his bar. 'Music draws a crowd,' he warns.

There is a solitary tap for Guinness. Every other type of drink comes out of a bottle. When he started, the Guinness came by train from St James's Gate. It was kept in wooden barrels that often leaked so the stout would rot. Fortunately, Guinness was always good for a refund. One thing Tom does not serve is póitín. He says there is good and bad póitín. 'Some people get a kind of madness,' he says, 'and if you drink water the next day, you'll get drunk again.'

He says the price of stout and whiskey stayed the same from 1920 to 1939. The pint was always nine-pence. Whiskey was ten-pence a half glass. 'The word "inflation" was never heard of until the war. Then things got dear and they got dearer ever since.'

Tom's one trip outside Ireland was a pilgrimage to Lourdes. That was in the days when the Catholic Church reigned supreme in Ireland. Although he would not consider himself a deeply religious man, he is nonetheless concerned for the fate of his faith. Its rapid decline became apparent to him when he attended the funeral of a popular priest in Limerick not long ago. He was astonished to note that of all the robed clerics that followed the hearse, not one was under fifty years of age. 'It's the same all over

131

Ireland,' he says. 'New people aren't coming forwards.' That is why he thinks the Church should update its thinking on marriage. 'It might mean those that went away from the Church would come back again,' he suggests. It is only a matter of time before the Church will be forced to give in on the subject. 'And they will have woman priests too!' he concludes. 'I have heard that discussed here umpteen times and ninety-nine per cent of people I know say priests should be allowed marry.'

Then again, he wonders was the collapse of the Church simply an inevitable consequence of prosperity? 'When people are poor, they are closer to God. When they are rich, they forget about him.'

MRS MARGARET SHORTT

Born 1925

Ladies Maid

Birr, County Offaly

Long centuries ago, Sir Laurence Parsons, brother of the Surveyor General of Ireland, acquired 1,000 acres of land in what was then the King's County. By the 1820s, Parsons' heirs had turned the old fortress into a sumptuous Gothic revival castle and built a bustling tree-lined town around it. Birr Castle remains the Parsons' family home today and its mighty walls engulf the handsome Georgian town where Cantonese chefs and Polish mechanics intermingle with the indigenous population.

Margaret Shortt lives in a small stone cottage close to the castle wall. For half a century, she slept within the castle itself. 'I had just turned seventeen when I started.' There was already eighteen staff in the household, including a butler and two footmen. 'The footmen wore green tailcoats, red waistcoats and big brass buttons. Even the soles of their shoes were shining!'

Margaret wore a khaki-coloured dress to signify her position as a ladies maid. As such, her role was to attend to all the chores necessary for her lady, especially when she hosted princesses or viscounts. Her immediate boss was 'the old Lady Rosse', a magnificent woman 'who dressed in the old style and knew all the Birr people and would wave if she saw you'. Lady Rosse's husband was the fifth Earl of Rosse, 'a beautiful old man', directly descended from Sir Laurence. Margaret's mother, a Miss O'Meara, left Birr as a young woman and secured a post as housemaid to the fun-loving McCalmonts of Mount Juliet, County Kilkenny. Here she met and married the McCalmonts' groom, a teacher's son called James Mackey. During the Troubles, James was shot at by the Black and Tans and he was obliged to lie low until the British army withdrew from Ireland. At length, he returned to Mount Juliet and remained their groom for the next forty-five years. The pride and joy of his stable was a powerful grey stallion called The Tetrarch, who was the Seabiscuit of Ireland during the First World War. 'My father looked after him every day. When we were kids, we used to go and watch him being washed. His tail was shampooed! He was a beautiful horse.'

Margaret was the second of the Mackeys six children. They lived in one of the McCalmonts cottages, close to where they kept the pack of hounds that headed up the Kilkenny Hunt. It was a good place to be a child. At Christmas, the McCalmonts threw large parties for all the children living on the estate.

'We used to have great craic. We'd not go to bed. They'd send us home with boxes of chocolate. That was a great thing!'

Although brought up in Mount Juliet, Margaret and her siblings often spent weeks on end back in Birr with their mother's mother. 'She only had two beds so we all had to share, the six of us.' Her grandmother's garden was awash with lavender and the evenings were long. She tells us this as we walk over to this house together. The building has been abandoned for some time and is up for sale. It looks at us with forlorn, sad eyes. Margaret shakes her head and we walk on.

Margaret Shortt believes the elderly are well looked after in Ireland. 'We have free travel. Free electricity, free heating, free briquettes. Free everything! They're very good to the blind too. I know people who have been in the dark all their life who are now looked after.'

While working in Birr Castle, Margaret met and married the late Pat Shortt, a cobbler from Birr who specialised in making 'the little lads' boots'. Their only son, John, is a barrister and lives in Blackrock, County Dublin, with his wife and two children. Margaret now lives with her younger sister, Sarah.

'The castle means an awful lot to me,' she says wistfully. 'It was a very good house for food and lots of posh, rich people came. I do miss it, the activity and everything. I still go walking in there a good deal.'

Birr has evolved a good deal in the eighty-one years since Margaret Shortt was born. It's likely to keep going that way. 'There's a lot of Chinese here now,' she says. 'They come to mass a good bit so they're good Catholics! And why not live here? Birr is a happy place!'

NELLIE O'TOOLE

Born 1908

Nurse & Housekeeper

Rathvilly, County Carlow, & Dublin

'People don't laugh as much as they should,' says Nellie suddenly. 'That's a shame – laughing is good for the heart.' When a ninety-seven-year-old woman says something like that, you are inclined to take notice. And despite all the sadness she must have witnessed, Nellie sure has a great laugh. It has a wonderful heart-rippling domino effect on all who hear it.

Nellie came to life in 1908 within the walls of a granite house on Rathvilly's Phelan Row. Rathvilly is a pretty village, situated by the River Slaney at the southern-most reaches of the Wicklow Mountains. Nellie's grandfather was the village cobbler. Her father, Peter O'Toole, was 'an ordinary man – he would work at anything he got'. They lived next door house to 'Granny Abbey' who lived to be 105. Nellie remembers her as 'always working in the garden at the back of the house'. She adored cooking. 'We used to go out and pick baskets of mushrooms,' recalls Nellie. 'Granny Abbey would boil the mushrooms then carefully strain the juice into four 'nice clean bottles'. She'd cork the bottles, then dig a hole in the garden, put down a bed of straw, lay the bottles to rest and cover it all with soil. A year later, she'd dig out the bottles and 'Oh my goodness,' says Nellie, 'the flavour was gorgeous.'

Shortly after Nellie's birth, her oldest brother, Tommy, emigrated to Chicago. In 1914, her brother Willy followed suit and took the steamer from Cobh to New York. In 1923, a third brother, Jimmy, did likewise. 'None of them ever came back,' says Nellie. But in the 1960s, she took the courageous step of flying out to see them. She stayed with Willy's family in California. Tommy and his wife took their first ever airplane journey to join her and stayed for four weeks. He hadn't seen Nellie since she was a baby. 'We had a great time,' chuckles Nellie. 'We had parties and everything. It was like they were all back in Ireland again, you know, when they started singing! Ah well, they're all gone now. I beat them all!'

While her brothers confronted life in the New World, young Nellie was learning how to cook and sew and make faces at the boys. At the summer fair, her sewing skills won her a pair of sandals. On Fridays, they'd follow the progress of the herring man and when he parped his horn they would shout out his name. 'The Herring Man! The Herring Man!' In summer, they'd cycle to the Fraughan Hills to collect blueberries which they ate 'in cup-loads'. In winters, they'd hide behind walls and watch the gentry dismount after a day's hunting. 'We'd know the names of them all.'

In the evenings, everyone would gather around to hear Nellie's mother read from the day's papers – Mr O'Callaghan, the Protestant minister, heard her reading once and said she had 'a wonderful voice'. 'He was a lovely man,' says Nellie. 'We'd be playing jackstones on the footpath and he'd want to know what we were at. We'd show him how to play and give him five stones and say, "Now!!" and the stones would all go flying!'

It wasn't all fun. Sometimes, after school, they had to go down to the corn mill by the river and remove all the old corn that was clogging the tiled floor. To this end, they were armed with knitting needles. But for all that, Nellie insists it was 'a wonderful life – you couldn't have better'.

However, dark clouds soon descended. In the winter of 1918, the Spanish Flu epidemic engulfed the planet and killed more than 20 million people. Rathvilly did not escape. Nellie says all thirteen houses on Phelan Row were hit. 'My mother said it was so bad my brother Jimmy was beating his head against the wall with it.' The only redemption came from 'the big house up above' at Lisnavagh where the Rathdonnells lived. 'At midday, every day, they sent down a big phaeton [an old fashioned pony and trap] with two men driving and two big churns of soup. Everyone would be out with their tubes and their cans and that. Boiling hot soup! Only for that, we were all gone.'

The flu had hardly abated before Ireland was plunged into its War of Independence. Again, Rathvilly was in the limelight. In November 1920, Kevin Barry, the eighteen-year-old son of one of the village's dairy queens, was arrested. Nellie knew him. 'He used to drive down to school in a little pony and trap every morning and leave it outside our house. Then he'd come on up to my mother at lunchtime'. In 1920, Kevin was ostensibly a happy, rugby-playing medical student at Belvedere College in Dublin, but he was also an active member of the IRA with several tactically brilliant ambushes under his belt. Nonetheless, his subsequent execution stunned everyone. 'The people in Rathvilly couldn't believe it,' says Nellie. 'We thought he might have been locked up – but to hang him like that!'

For the rest of the war, Rathvilly became a focal point for the British military. 'The troubled times were very bad here,' says Nellie. 'At night, we'd see soldiers flashlights coming in from Baltinglass. They'd come in their big, noisy lorries and take over the schoolyard. They'd go through all the houses, demanding to know, "Who have you in bed? Have you any men here?" Any men they found would have to get up out of bed and give answers. Sometimes they'd be taken away and given a beating. It was shocking really.'

Nellie's brother, Jimmy, was mad about many things, but most especially cars. One wet evening, he told his mother he had to go.

'When?

'Now.'

'Who with?'

'I can't say.'

He was escorting Michael Collins down to Cork. In 1923, Jimmy settled in the city of Carbondale, Illinois. He joined the American army but died young. His coffin was covered in an American flag which was sent home to Nellie as his next of kin.

As for Nellie, she left Rathvilly for Dublin when she was sixteen and found work as a nurse at the Jockey Hospital on the Curragh. She subsequently moved to England to work at the Moneyhull Colony in Solihull. In 1945, she became housekeeper to a bank manager working in Sligo. When his wife died shortly afterwards, Nellie stayed on to help raise his baby daughter, Georgina. In turn, Georgina and her son now keep a close eye on Nellie in her Dublin home.

Nellie plans to stay around until she's met the president and scooped the Centenarian's Bounty. She puts her longevity down to the fact that she has a cup of Barry's tea first thing every morning, two sugars and a dash of milk. Oh yes, and a good hearty laugh.

JACK O'NEILL

Born 1925

Builder

Tuckmill Cross, County Wicklow

It's hard to know just how 'rough' Jack's gang was. He suggests they were 'as rough a crowd as there was in Ireland'. But his stories of the gang tend to concern the twenty of them, Jack's five brothers included, meeting at Tuckmill Cross in the summer for a game of football or maybe pitch 'n' toss or perhaps a crack at the skittles. They did frequently clamber over the wall into the orchard of the nearby Saunders Grove estate to steal a few apples, and there is much talk of gambling and cards, but he only tells of one occasion when they came before the law. He and a brother chanced upon some fellows from Mayo who were causing a rumpus outside Quinn's Pub in Baltinglass. Jack swears his brother was simply counselling them to pipe down when one lad started rolling up his sleeves for a fight. 'Oh be the holy!' recalls Jack delightedly of the subsequent brawl, 'You should have heard them squeal!' However, the advantage ultimately went the way of Mayo when a garda with 'a bone to pick' arrived on the scene. 'We were fined thirty bob each and bound to the peace for a year.' Sixty-odd years later, Jack still can't help smarting that the Mayo lads got away scot-free.

Jack was the third and smallest of the O'Neill brothers – 'but I wasn't the softest, no way'. He was born at Tuckmill in a house his father rented from Saunders Grove for £25 a year. The house was built as a pub for farmers coming to and from the weekly Baltinglass Fair. It had been the scene of a violent murder some years before he was born when a woman shot her husband as he came down the stairs. 'We all used to hear him coming down the stairs again or pushing milk jugs over. You'd think someone was after leaving in the cat but then you'd look and, by the curse of God, there wouldn't be a cat anywhere.' Jack says all this very matter-of-factly. His sympathies clearly lie with the ghost. Perhaps, he suggests, the poor ghost might strike up a fancy with the unfortunate servant girl who 'got in trouble' with old Colonel Saunders and was duly bumped off by the gardener. 'I often heard people saying her screams could be heard all along the river valley once a year.'

Tuckmill was a lively place for a young fellow. Twice a day the Sallins to Tullow train would rattle through the fields behind the house, 'By jayzus when the midday train went past, even the horses knew that meant dinner time!' On Tuesday mornings, the brothers watched the mountain farmers coming down from the Glen of Imaal to drive their cattle and sheep to the fair in Baltinglass. At weekends, they would sometimes cycle up to Dublin to watch a match in Croke Park. 'We'd go as far as Tallaght, then throw our old bikes down anywhere we liked and get the tram into the Pillar. The bikes would still be there when we come back. But now they'd have it gone before you leave it down.'

One of the more traumatic episodes in Jack's life occurred when his baby brother toddled into a field of corn that their father was cutting at the time with a horse-drawn harvester. 'The foot was cut straight across the ankle and how he didn't cut the two of them, no one will ever know.' Jack carried his brother's severed foot home. By fortune, a neighbour in the Irish Guards, on leave from England, was passing in his car. He pulled off his shirt, wrapped it around the leg to stem the blood and sped off to hospital with Jack's brother and father. Jack, left holding the severed foot, started for home. 'I was only six year old and I didn't know the differ.' A herdsman from Cavan called Larry Smith found Jack at the bridge and took the foot. 'That was the last I saw of it.' As for his brother, 'He lived to be a tough and contrary fellow – I often said they cut the wrong end of him!' He had a leg made for him by a mechanic in Baltinglass and learned to ride a bike by using a cocoa tin for a pedal.

Jack, recalling his schooldays in Baltinglass, spoke of daily brutality that was not uncommon. 'The head teacher would slap us from morning to night. There were three other teachers in it but the only nice one was Mr Doyle and he died of TB.' Moreover, everything was taught in Irish, a language Jack struggled to grasp. 'And I'd say eighty per cent of the 200 lads who were at that school went to England during the war where their Irish wasn't worth a feck.' Jack's oldest brother was among those who emigrated.

When he was fourteen years old, Jack began work as an apprentice builder to his father. Together, they built a sawmill and some sheds for Mr O'Neill's fledgling timber business. Then they moved on to building cottages. His father was an excellent teacher and made sure all his sons worked hard. 'We were workers all back along the line,' says Jack proudly. 'Work was no trouble to us.'

By 1945, Jack was in a position to set up his own building business. 'I started with one old Major tractor after the war and I made a trailer. I paid for the tractor within a year but I tell you, there was feck all in the building at that time. The lad filling potholes on the road made as much as a builder in that time. And I had to rear eleven children on it.'

The house that Jack built for his wife, Sheila, and their eleven children is one of perhaps twenty houses in counties Wicklow and Carlow he constructed. It is located within full view of Tuckmill Cross where he and the boys used to gather on summer's evenings. Most of his brothers are dead now but Jack is still to the good, shifting from philosophical ponderings on modern warfare to heartbreakingly funny reminiscences. Every Sunday, he rambles up to the village of Grangecon for a pint in Mrs Moore's establishment. 'It's good to get out for an old chat. I'll go while I'm able because I'm going to be dead long enough.'

MICHAEL BRENNAN ROE

Born 1937

Coalminer

Castlecomer, County Kilkenny

Michael holds out his miner's hands, still etched with pallid blue stains from where coal dust got into the inevitable cuts. 'You hear a lot of talk these days about child labour in Asia and Africa,' he says quietly, 'but it wasn't so long ago they had it here in Kilkenny.' In 1951, a few weeks after his fourteenth birthday, Michael Brennan Roe made his first trip down into the dark wet tunnels of the Deerpark coalmines in Castlecomer. Coal dust was in the blood. 'My father, grandfather and great-grandfather were miners on both sides and my uncles and brother too.'

For the next eighteen years, Michael headed down, six days a week, living the intensely claustrophobic existence of a coal miner, eight hours a day, Monday through Friday, and five hours on a Saturday. 'In the winters, we'd see no sunlight until Sunday.'

The Comer Mines were founded in the 1740s by the Prior-Wandesforde family. By the late nineteenth century, the famous smokeless anthracite was heating homes throughout the British Isles. By the 1950s, the coal seams were proving too narrow for modern technology and the Wandesfordes were still trying to maintain a workforce of 500 men.

'There's a few older than me left,' says Michael, 'but not so many now.' One of them is Paddy Love, a cobbler living in the hills outside Clogh who specialises in dancing shoes. Paddy is pushing eighty-four but keeps his hair black as the coal he mined as a youth. 'Don't mention it!' he says with a grimace. 'It was terrible. Pure slavery!' The reaction is the same for most of those who remember the mines although there are some who insist the craic was mighty and that it was simply a way of life.

Michael was 'trained in' by Mark Brennan, an old collier who'd been mining since before the First World War. Mark literally taught him how to lie on his side and hack coal off the narrow seams. 'You learned quickly what not to do. You couldn't whistle or sing because you're dependent on your hearing. Or sit on your haunches in case a rock fell and landed on your legs out flat. You really needed to have platinum legs.'

Michael's first major job was as a hauler – 'letting down empty tubs and pulling up the coal' – then transferring the tubs to a donkey and cart which would take them on to the coal-train. Mark showed him how 'to load up trucks with anything up to half a ton of coal and push it off up the tracks'. 'There was switching around as you got older – if you got a name as a fearless one, you got the jobs.' The hardest job was that of the contract trammers – 'the men that were pushing the trams' – if you gave them a hand 'they might give you a few bob or some fags'.

During the 1930s, a Communist group headed by Nixie Boran formed a union that, ultimately, won some improvements to the miners' welfare. But even in Michael's time, injuries were commonplace and accidental deaths not unusual. 'If the buzzer sounded for fifteen minutes that meant someone had been killed.' The only wildlife they encountered were the rats who urinated in the water and stole their food. 'Conditions were very bad down there,' says Michael. He spoke of inhaling gelignite and coal dust all day long, of men and boys spluttering with chronic coughs and shortness of breath. 'There was always talk about getting good air into the mines but that was put on the long finger.' The incidence of emphysema, bronchitis and pneumoconiosis (black lung disease) were high and, after nearly two decades down there, Michael did not escape. He had to have part of a lung removed. 'It was a strange thing but we never had any fear. We weren't afraid of getting hurt.'

The Castlecomer mines finally closed on 31 January 1969. Today, all that remains are the ruins of an old bath house where the miners took their showers and a massive pyramid of coal dust over which cattle now graze. Michael was amongst the last to leave. 'I don't think there was anyone too sad bar maybe those making their living out of supplying miners with food and all that.' He then went on to work at the Comerama Textile Mill in Castlecomer.

'Once you're able to throw the two feet out of the side of bed in the morning, you're not too bad.' He lives in Castlecomer with his wife, Lizzie, the mother of their five children. Michael is a quiet, intelligent man with a healthy appetite who believes that life is a good deal better today than it was in the past – although he just cannot stomach televisions in pubs. He also finds it frustrating to describe the way it was in the Comer Mines to today's teenagers. 'Either they don't understand or they don't believe me! But I was down there and I seen how it was.'

KATHLEEN LYNAM
& KATHLEEN KEOGH

Born 1930 & 1925
House Parlour Maid & Factoryworker
Kiltegan, County Wicklow

'At the end of it all, I'm just a jackeen from the Coombe,' says Kathleen Keogh. The words elicit a hearty chuckle from her younger cousin, Kathleen Lynam. The two Kathleens have known each other since the summers of their childhood when the jackeen was dispatched south to spend some time with her kinsfolk in the Wicklow Mountains. The Keoghs were blacksmiths and they had forges in Talbotstown, Graigue and just outside the village of Kiltegan.

John Keogh, the man of the house, died young in 1937 and Bridget, his widow, was left with two small sons, Jack and Peter, and a little daughter, Kathleen. Bridget was a capable woman. She got on with the show and raised her children – and their visiting cousin – as best she could.

'It's amazing to think of her now,' says Kathleen Lynam of her mother. 'And what she did for us. It was a different world. There was no taps, no sinks, no nothing. We only had a few oil lamps. We done our homework by candlelight. We got our water from the well and we ate our meals on stools. We always had porridge for breakfast, big plates of porridge, with lots of goats milk.'

Bridget kept a vegetable garden and excelled at making bread and currant cakes. 'Once a week, she would walk the seven miles to Baltinglass with a basket on her arm and come home with some beef. There wouldn't be any luxuries, mind you,' laughs Kathleen. 'But there might be colcannon. Potatoes and cabbage all mixed together, make a well in the middle and put a big lump of butter in it … ah, we used to love that!'

Kiltegan was a happy place to be a child. They played road-skittles and pitch 'n' toss. They milked cows and hid in the woods. They rowed the lakes of Humewood in 'leaky boats'. When they got out on the lake, Kathleen Lynam – 'the only girl amongst eight or nine lads' – would be given 'an auld rusty bean tin' and instructed to fish all the water out. 'I got no sympathy,' she says. 'I was just a skivvy.'

When they weren't on the lake, they were clambering up the old Round Tower. Its rotten stairs still make her shudder today. 'I don't know how we ever made it to the top.' Although raised as Catholics, the children were not discouraged from mingling with their Protestant neighbours. 'We had as much fun with them as we did with anybody,' she says. 'And that's the way it should be. I was never able to understand why people made such a thing about the difference. We're all talking to the same God.'

In time, Kathleen's son Peter took on the family forge. 'The Keoghs were always blacksmiths,' he says. 'They shod every horse that ever passed through the Glen of Imaal.' They were 'tenant blacksmiths', or farriers, to the Hume family. They paid their rent by shoeing the Hume's hunters and they made their living shoeing for everybody else. Much of the metalwork at Humewood was crafted here – gates, fences, fire-grids, grain forks and such like. Peter says his grandfather was 'an exceptionally contrary old man'. 'No one could sledge right for him – except the wife. She had to do all the sledging for him!'

Most forges have a clay floor. The Keogh's one was made from wood so that the draught horses could come in and crush the coal nuggets into smaller, more heat sensitive chips. The wooden floor had an added bonus. 'Nobody had electricity then – and a warm house could be scarce enough.' With the fire burning, the Forge offered heat, light – and entertainment. 'A lad with an accordion would get the dancing going,' recalls Kathleen, who hosted a dance here after her marriage in 1949 to John Keogh. 'We'd only ever have half-sets; there wasn't room for a full set. But that was where all the courting was done!'

And it was done without drink. The Keoghs are Pioneers. They took the pledge at their confirmation and have never tasted wine nor stout in their lives. 'I never tried to stop my own children from drinking,' says Kathleen, talking about her ten children, 'although I have one granddaughter now who is a Pioneer too.'

Dancing at the forge faded out in the 1950s with the emergence of purpose-built venues like the Parish Hall and Village Hall. The local priest was also eager to keep a close eye on his courting flock. In the 1970s, the GAA revitalised set dancing with their SCOR programme. A teacher came up from Wexford to remind everyone how it was done. Today, set dancing takes place in the Kiltegan Town Hall every Tuesday night and the Blacksmith's Reel is still among the more popular tunes.

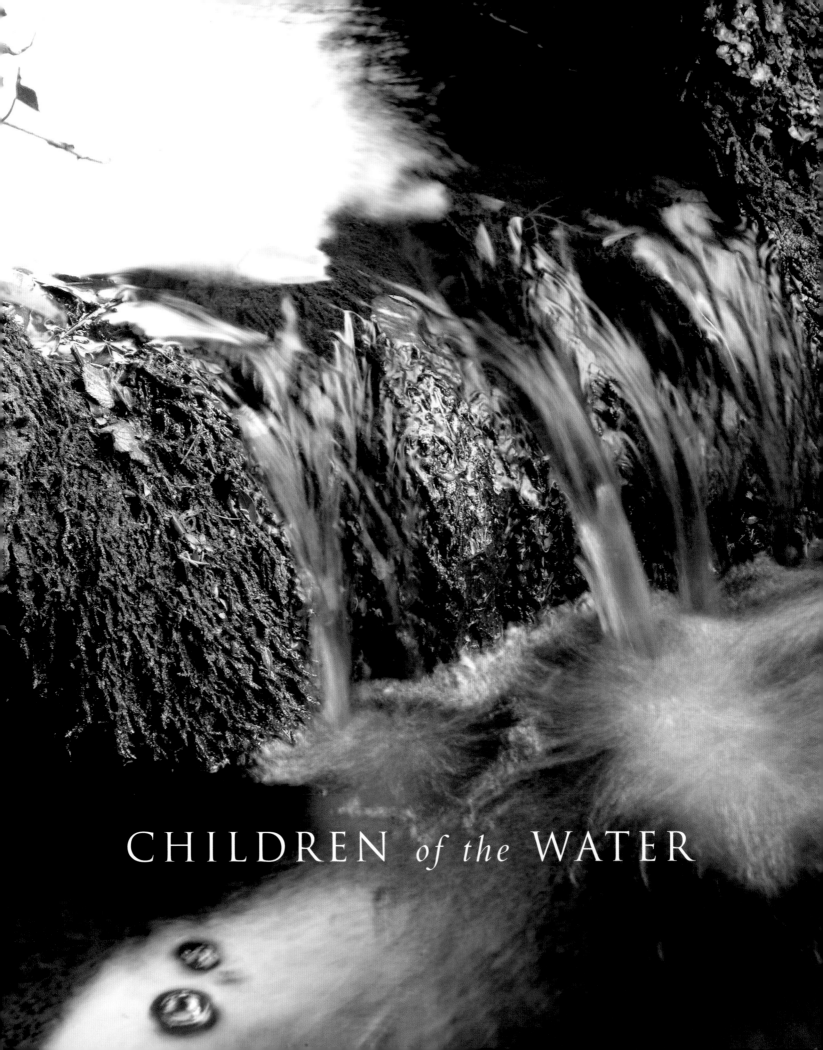

CHILDREN *of the* WATER

FRANK MAHER

Born 1936

Fisherman & Carpenter

The River Blackwater, Doneraile, County Cork

There are those who believe an angler is a man who enjoys sitting on muddy riverbanks doing nothing because he can't get away with doing nothing at home. But for Mary Maher, knowing that her husband was casting his rod in the River Blackwater was certainly preferable to the prospect of him sinking a heap of pints in the village. 'If I'd stayed here until morning, she'd have been happy,' says Frank. 'Just so long as I wasn't in the pub!'

Mary, reared in Doneraile, northwest Cork, was working as a housekeeper and Frank was working as a carpenter on the power stations in England when they met. From the age of twelve, he had served his apprenticeship with a great-uncle in Mallow. Frank's Waterford-born father was in charge of driving the sugar beet in from Mallow train station to the factory.

In 1952, fifteen-year-old Frank went 'on my own' to England and began working on the Aldermaston power station outside Reading. He swiftly became part of an Irish gang that roamed around England, living in camps and hostels, working on the power stations and tearing off ration stamps for their breakfast, lunch and tea. By the time he married in June 1956, he'd become a foreman.

Frank and Mary returned to Ireland in 1960. Mary concentrated on raising their children, six boys and four girls, and Frank headed off around Ireland with his toolbox in pursuit of an income. One of his first commissions was to build the Rippon piano factory in Shannon. He then worked with McInernys on the construction of a new jet runway at Shannon airport to accommodate the first long-range jets, like the Boeing 720, that had begun operating on the route. Frank remembers it well, 'It was exciting to see these new planes coming in.' By the 1970s, he was working on housing developments in Limerick, Galway and Tallaght.

'I'm a carpenter by trade but I'm retired now,' says Frank. 'When you get over seventy, you may throw the towel in and go fishing.' The last carpentry job Frank did was to gather a load of pine logs, bring them to the south bank of the Blackwater and turn them into a cabin. Elevated on sturdy stilts four feet above ground, the cabin is safely out of harm's way should the river burst its banks. The walls are lined with newspaper clippings, rods, boots, thank you letters, photographs, birds nests, chain saws and other notices. A photograph displays the biggest fish he ever caught, a twenty-two-pounder. The view from the cabin is of a fine wrought iron bridge – which Frank also built – across the Blackwater and, on the horizon, a horse-filled paddock, an old limekiln and a tree-lined avenue leading to an old Norman castle.

The cabin is Frank's base for his present career as a ghillie. He began nearly twenty years ago and now looks after those guests from Ballyvolane House outside Castlelyons who come to enjoy this fantastic two-mile beat. He enjoys the role very much and has met many remarkable people from politicians and aristocrats, to surgeons and lawyers. 'They're all normal when they get here,' he says, 'although you'd have to watch the language … well, until they get to know you and then you can carry on!'

There can be no doubting that if Frank put ten cents in a box every time he swore, he'd probably be able to buy Latvia by now and, as it happens, if Frank could live anywhere else, it would most likely be Latvia. One of his sons-in-law owns a lakeside property out there and, on a recent visit, Frank was much taken with the country, declaring it to be 'way ahead of Ireland'. He was particularly taken by a crèche full of mini motor cars so that 'the little ones learn how to use gears and indicators and all that'.

Much to Frank's amusement, Mary never learned to fish. 'She knew everything there was to know about fishing, the times, the winds, what flies and what rods to use – but she never did the fishing.'

Mary passed away in May 2005, just a month before she and Frank would have celebrated their Golden Wedding Anniversary. In her latter years, she had worked at the gift shop in Croom Mills. Frank misses her terribly, though he draws much warmth from the fact that they have thirty-seven grandchildren and six great-grandchildren. Today, Frank's preferred spot is to be on his lonesome, waist deep in the river, listening to the breeze rustle through cow parsley and ragwort, the gloop of a passing fish, the bark of a distant dog, the rushing of the waters. Before she died, Mary made one last request – that he would not go back to the pub. 'And I didn't,' says Frank. 'They thought I would, but I didn't. And I wouldn't go back now.'

JOHN COONEY

Born 1922

Postman & Carpenter

Achill Island

John Cooney is the oldest man in Achill Sound. And aside from 104-year-old Bridget Gallagher, he is the oldest on the island. From 1939 to 1958, he was the Sound's postman. You see him walking around, a tall man in sporty shirt, tie and woolly hat. A slight limp, hands behind back. He's eighty-four, well-read, insightful and kind. He lives in a Roadmaster cabin pitched between a toy shop and a 250-year-old building that belonged to his mother's family, the Corrigans. Within a minute of meeting him, he has hopped into the back of our car and said, 'You met the right man! I've nothing else to do and I'm sober. Come on and I'll show you around.'

John was born on 14 June 1922, the only child to a sheep-farming couple on Achill. His father's father lived on the nearby island of Achill Beg, electrified but deserted since, while a great-grandfather by name of Hanue came from Inisturk, off Clew Bay. 'I don't know where they came from before then. The family call themselves Heaney now.'

Young John was educated in a three-teacher school in the Sound, since closed. For the first eleven years of his life, he spoke only Irish – the Achill dialect – but he 'picked up the English quick enough' as a teenager. His expanding mind was nourished by a near exclusive diet of seafood. 'I didn't know hardly a thing about meat when I was young. It was all fish. We had the real breakfast in the morning. The egg would be warm after the hen laying it.

Although Achill prospered in the early nineteenth century, from the 1840s famine and emigration dragged the island into a downward spiral that lasted 150 years. Captain Boycott, the Achill Island land agent who inspired the expression 'to boycott', was one of many who felt the pinch. The population tumbled from its peak of 8,000 and today rests at about 3,000. Many islanders headed west, via Cobh, to America. Large droves found their way to Cleveland, Ohio. 'That became the passage of assistance,' says John, 'and it became an Achill stronghold. I had two aunts and an uncle that went there and I have cousins there now. One of them sent a text over to McLoughlin's [his local pub] wishing me a Happy Easter!'

In the 1930s, a closer option for summer work was Scotland. All the young lads would catch the train from Achill to Dublin and then head up to the tattie fields around Glasgow. John shows us a Celtic

Cross, erected in Kildavnet Cemetery in September 1937, to mark the resting spot of ten of these unfortunate boys, killed in a fire at the village of Kirkintillock. 'I was at school with them,' he says. 'Most were related to me. They weren't fourteen years of age. They were classed as muck, poor devils. Picking potatoes. Someone set fire to them. They were locked in from the outside. The Mannions lost three sons at the once. It was an awful calamity. Their coffins came in on the train and that was the last train that ever came to Achill Sound.' Across from their grave is the hollow ruin of Granuaile's Castle. 'Wasn't it changed times since?' says John quietly, looking at the castle.

John Cooney did not emigrate. His parents were getting older so, as the only child, he stayed. 'My mother ran a bed and breakfast so I would help her with that. We were fairly well off. They never wanted to see me going.' In 1939, he secured work as the Achill Sound postman. 'I was eighteen years when I started! I had to cycle to all the villages. Or walk. By God, I was fit as a fiddle!' He swam – 'like a fish' – and a priest taught him how to box. He cycled everywhere on his Raleigh, sometimes as far as Croagh Patrick which he'd climb for the day and then cycle home again afterwards, 'no bother'. In summer evenings, he and his friends would climb the island's summits to behold the leisurely sunsets. In 1942, he played centre half-back for Achill when they won the Mayo Championship – 'And I'm the only one left of that team still alive!' Four years later, he cycled 150 miles to Tuam to watch Mayo lose to Roscommon in the Connaught championship final.

After the war, John was obliged to head east for England every autumn to work for a few months. 'It's not what you know but who you know. Lads from over here were in charge over there so you'd find work quick enough. I used to be counting the days until Christmas. In Irish they say "*níl aon tinteán le do thinteán féin*" – "there's no fireplace like your own fireplace".'

In 1959, he stopped being a postman and secured regular work as a carpenter on the vast power stations of Wales – 'where the sheep were small and the cattle had horns six feet wide!' At the steelworks in Newport, he was one of 600 Irishmen working all the hours God sent. These were rowdy years for John but all that changed when JFK was shot on 22 November 1963. 'I didn't drink for a long time after that. It was a terrible thing to happen. A big shock. He will be remembered for all time.'

Instead, he returned home to look after his mother permanently. 'I stayed with her all the time. She went into the wheelchair in the finish. Otherwise, I'd have been married and gone away.' She died in January 1972 and his father passed away that July. 'My mother always said, "When you're in England, always go to mass." When I miss a mass, I think of her.'

As we make our way west across the once-sandy roads of the island, we pass endless abandoned stone cottages. John tells us these were all thatched in his youth with oftentimes ten children to a bed. 'The thatch was very warm but it was cool in summertime. The birds would nest in the roof in the spring. They kept the home fires going all year round for the cooking. The fires never went out on Achill.'

These blind, scalped ruins stand at odds with the shimmering new developments of the present generation. 'All these houses are holiday homes,' he sighs. 'You'd think we had a great population but nobody's actually living there.' Our journey takes us through a landscape of treacherous bogs, contrary bends, plunging cliffs, flourishing gorse and mighty mountains. At length we reach Moyteoge Head over Keem Strand. 'Well lads,' says John, 'there's nothing between here and America but the Atlantic Ocean.'

MICHAEL KING

1925–2006

Politician, Postmaster & Farmer

Errislannan, Connemara

When Michael King was born, the Errislannan peninsula in Connemara probably didn't look a whole lot different to the way it looks today. Of course, there would have been a few more stone cottages in the 1920s, the last traces of the homes once occupied by the tenants of the island's four landlords. One of these landlords was John Byrne, Collector General of Rates in Dublin in about 1850. 'He owned property all around Wicklow, Dublin and Galway,' says Mickey. 'But he lost the job in Dublin through some fiddle. They were tough times but I suppose he wasn't bad as landlords go.' And as landlords go, he went. Michael does not say that the Kings numbered among Byrne's thirty tenant families. Instead, he says that the Kings have been on Errislannan forever.

They certainly held the Post Office for a long time. Michael's grandmother became postmistress of Errislannan in 1871. In time, she was succeeded by her son who was in turn succeeded by his nephew, Michael. That latter transition took place in 1946 and, for the next fifty-seven years, Michael was centre stage to all activity on the peninsula. In 2004, An Post closed the office citing too little business and so brought to an end 133 years of King dominance.

A quiet, philosophical man, Michael was born in what has now become a summer house for a Dublin family. He was the oldest of six children. His brother and four sisters were all to the good when we met him. Their father was a 'fifty-acre farmer'.

Michael built the house where he and his wife live over fifty years ago. 'I carted all the stones for it here on a horse and cart.' In a small field next to his birthplace, he keeps a magnificent pedigree Charolais bull by name of Sam. 'I've farmed all my life,' he says. 'Although it wasn't farming really – it was slavery!'

Among Mickey's possessions is a thank you letter from Bertie Ahern. It relates to his service as President of the Thomas Whelan Cumann in Clifden. The cumann is named for one of Michael Collins' trusted men, a young Connemara volunteer who was captured by the British after Bloody Sunday and hanged in March 1921. Shortly after the execution, the local IRA gunned down two Royal Irish Constables in Clifden and, on St Patrick's Day, the Black and Tans retaliated by burning fourteen houses in the area, killing one civilian and wounding another. Mickey says the presence of the Tans in Connemara had a powerful effect in fanning the flames of revolt. 'They were jailbirds and they let them loose here, right into the islands. They were given guns and told to shoot the Irish down if need be.' Not surprisingly, the people of Connemara have a high regard for General Tom Barry and 'the boys of north Cork' who waged the most effective resistance to the Black and Tans within Ireland.

'Then the Civil War came,' says Michael sadly. 'Brother against brother. Collins was told, "Take that or prepare for immediate and terrible war." What answer had they? They were on their knees! But the country split and so did every house in Ireland. Collins' crowd became Cumann na Gael and later became Fine Gael. De Valera's became Fianna Fáil. They haven't made friends yet!'

Michael says it is astonishing how the bitterness still rises after all this time, especially at election time. He wondered if the divisions will ever heal. However, as the number of Eastern European migrants to Connemara escalates, he concedes that such 'old world' perspectives might change rapidly in the coming decades.

Michael has the physical look of a wrestler. In younger years, he cycled a good deal and fished for salmon and lobster on the waters of Mannin Bay. He says there was no hurling or football on the peninsula. 'It didn't get this far! Anyway, if you were from here, you'd never get onto the county team ... the east Galway fellows would never pass you a ball!'

He and Mrs King, a Ballyconeely girl, have two daughters and two sons. One of his sons is on target for a place in *The Guinness Book of Records*. Gerard King has played prop with the Connemara All-Blacks for the past twenty-three years. 'He'd be gone three years ago,' explains his father, 'but they haven't found anyone to replace him!'

Michael remains astonished by Ireland's new-found opulence. As with many of us, it just wasn't a circumstance he considered possible. There are, of course, downsides to the boom. He calculates that for every occupied house on Errislannan, there are five holiday homes. 'But it's better to have them that way than in ruins.'

He is also wary of those who insist everyone is prospering. 'Tourism is blown up to be a great shape in these parts but its not really. Outside Clifden, the B&Bs have gone to the wall these last few years.' He says the clamp down on drinking and driving has had a major effect. 'We used to go out on the long winters nights for five or six pints. We'd drink them slow, then drive home after. Now the pubs are all empty and people stay at home with a takeout. If you're not within walking distance of the pubs, you may forget it. I can see the point of it, but it has killed country life definitely. Any place you have to drive to is affected. But I suppose there's no other answer.'

Michael King passed away in June 2006.

WILLY & PAT 'RUA' REILLY

Born 1914 & 1907

Fishermen

Glenlara, Belmullet, County Mayo

At six o'clock on the evening of Friday, 28 October 1927, Pat 'Rua' Reilly put to sea in his canvas covered curragh. The boys were heading out to catch some mackerel and Pat was not going to miss out. The day had been stormy but the winds were now quiet and the ocean calm. Pat's brothers, Teddy and Sean, were in another curragh. There were thirty men in total. An hour or so after they set off, the winds began to pick up. Some of the older fishermen began to feel uneasy and turned for home, Pat amongst them. At seven-thirty, a hurricane struck. 'It came like a shot out of a gun,' says Pat, 'and I am the only man still alive who came back that night.' The storm devastated the west coast of Ireland. Forty-five fishermen lost their lives – including ten of Pat's men. Sean's body was found the next day. Teddy's came in the day after. 'They were all young men.' says Pat. "Sean was twenty-two and Teddy was fourteen.'

'The Drowning', as it became known, marked the end of an era for the two islands of Inishkea where the men had lived. They lie just off County Mayo's Mullet Peninsula. Pat and Willie's parents were both islanders – his father from the north island and his mother from the south. 'The Reillys came from Cavan,' says Pat, 'so God knows why they were in Inishkea!' His mother's family were easier to explain. 'My grandfather was an O'Donnell from Galway. He came down fishing with a crowd and met a girl and married her and he stayed on after.'

The Reillys were one of six families who lived on the south island, each one in a stone cottage. Pat was born there on 18 August 1907. 'The island was a nice place to live,' he recalled. 'We had lots of holiday-makers then.' Pat started fishing when he was twelve – 'and I was fishing all my life since'. The community spoke Irish and everyone kept chickens and grew potatoes, cabbage and turnips. They had little need for money except to buy flour, sugar and tea. The boys hurled using sea-rods and Pat remembers playing a football match against the Belmullet boys – and beating them! There was a small pub on the north island and a shebeen on the south. 'A priest used to come out twice a year and stay in our house.' Otherwise, the islanders dutifully said the Rosary by themselves every Sunday.

As is often the case with neighbours, the two islands took opposing sides during the Irish Civil War. 'The south went Fine Gael and the north went Fianna Fáil,' says Pat with a smile. 'We'd throw stones

169

across and we had guns on each other but we were all right after that. We'd have a dance on one island the one night and the next Sunday we'd all be over on the other.'

After 'The Drowning', the shattered community began to seek land on the mainland. 'We had to leave,' said Pat, who was twenty-one at the time. 'The land was against us. There was too much seaweed on it.' The Land Commission responded by settling them on small holdings with new houses adjacent to their old fishing grounds. They were also allowed to retain their houses and lands on the islands. Most were settled at Glosh on the coast of Blacksod Bay. In 1933, Pat and his younger brother Willie were relocated to Glenlara at the very tip of Erris Head. This is where the two brothers live today, their handsome houses separated by a small field.

The landscape of Erris is bleak and confounding. Even the rivers have sunk into the bog. It's the sort of place where you'd want to like your neighbours. But the Reilly brothers seem to enjoy living there. Pat did a stint of coast-watching in Howth during the war. 'Keeping an eye on things!' he says. But he preferred the west coast to the east.

Eight years Pat's junior, Willie is a tall man with a booming voice who likes to read. He was too young to be out on the night of 'The Drowning'. But he says Erris is not a whole lot different to Inishkea. 'We had to learn English, but we picked it up not too bad anyhow.'

Two years after he settled in Glenlara, Pat married Mary Macandra, from Bellagarvaun. They were together almost seventy years before Mary passed away in August 2005. 'She was a great woman,' says Pat. They had twelve children – eight sons and four daughters – who are scattered from the hills of Donegal to the coast of Australia. The girls are all nurses. 'One of my lads is dead,' Pat says. 'John-Joe – he died in England, killed himself with drink.' Pat says he was a drinker in his youth but took the pledge over fifty years ago. 'I never got a penny of dole or nothing,' he explains. 'So you needed your wits to raise a big family.'

Pat shows me a photograph of a family reunion where he sits like Queen Victoria amid a tribe of his sixty grandchildren, twenty great-grandchildren and four great-greats.

Willie was not far behind. In 1944, he married a girl called Marianne Lavelle thirteen years his junior, who was also born on the islands. Their five boys and three girls already have twenty children between them – however, Marianne sadly passed away in January 2006.

The Reilly blood is clearly a virulent solution. Willie is ninety-two and reads without glasses. Pat is ninety-eight and still knows how to wink. A sister who went to America in 1928 turns 103 over Christmas 2006.

Today the Inishkea islands are home to sheep, cattle, seals and Ireland's largest population of barnacle geese. Its weather station served a useful role in advising the allies of weather conditions during the Second World War. The Reillys still own land out there and Pat's son brings sheep out on a boat. A neighbour, whose father also left the island in the 1930s, tells us the brothers are the only men alive who really remember what the islands were like. 'They might be still out there but for 'The Drowning',' he says.

TOM CONNOLLY

Born 1917

Boat Driver & Engineman

Rathangan, County Kildare

Tom Connolly is one of the legends of the Grand Canal. For many long decades, the eighty-nine-year-old from Shannon Harbour was to be seen guiding barges to and fro along the inland waterways of Ireland.

Tom was the third last of 'six lads and three girls' born to James Connolly, the lock-keeper at Shannon Harbour during the first decades of the twentieth century. Shannon Harbour was built in 1830 to provide a link between the horse-drawn barges that came up the Grand Canal from Dublin and the various boats that serviced the towns and villages along the Shannon.

The town had a bonded warehouse, a customs and excise post and a Royal Irish Constabulary barracks complete with holding cells. There was the Harbour Masters house, a boat repair dockyard, a school, several taverns, a smithy and livery, a large number of stone cottages and a Grand Hotel.

For Tom and his siblings, it was a wonderful place to be 'raised and reared'. They learned to swim in the three waters that gathered at the harbour – namely the Grand Canal itself and the rivers Shannon and Brosna. There were corncrakes to watch and fish to be caught. Handball was a particular favourite of Tom's although he also had a strong penchant for dancing.

Indeed, it was the day after a dance that Tom's barge, laden with beet, clunked to a halt outside Rathangan. 'It was 19 and 40', says Tom. 'At that time, the war was on and the government used to store a lot of beet in Rathangan. We had pulled in at Spenser's Bridge and that's where I first saw the lady herself.'

'Wasn't I the fortunate one!' interjects Joan, preparing tea and biscuits behind us. Joan Conlan had also grown up on the canal. Indeed, like Tom, she and her twelve siblings had swum its waters, admired its birds, played hide and seek amid its leafy banks. They lived near the Spenser Bridge outside Rathangan, in a small cottage built by their father in 1908.

A friend of Joan's was engaged in a secret romance with one of Tom's colleagues on the boats. Fearful that her family would disapprove of a liaison with a boatman, the friend had asked Joan to deliver a message for her. Joan cycled down to the boat and tapped on the window. Lo and behold, Tom looked up and said, 'Sure, where did you come out from?'

'And that was that', they say in virtual unison.

Tom had left school in 1933 and spent the subsequent year 'minding the locks' for his father, opening and closing the gates to level the water. 'There was a kind of farm out the back as well so there was cattle to look after and hay to be got and turf to be got too.' However, by the early 1930s, the horse-drawn boats, once so popular in Shannon Harbour, were giving way to diesel-fuelled barges that could make their way directly to the Shannon quays. Shannon Harbour had become little more than a toll booth and refuelling depot. Young Tom grew restless. 'I always wanted to work on the canal,' he explains. 'So, my eldest brother came home and took over the lock and I started on the boats in 1935.'

For the next twenty years, Tom helped steer countless motorised barges along Ireland's waterways. One of his most frequent missions was to bring Guinness from Dublin to the West. This involved loading up a barge with anything up to 450 kegs at James Street, behind the brewery, and then voyaging west 131 kilometres to his childhood home at Shannon Harbour. From there, they would often keep going south down the Shannon to Limerick.

'There was a long run and a short run,' explains Tom. 'On the long run, you'd go on to the Shannon and that'd give you a few days rest. On the shorter run, you'd go by Tullamore. But you wouldn't ever know when you'd get back. Some of the drink might not be so good when we got there,' says Tom with a smile. 'But I never touched them. I never drank in my life.'

On the journey back to Dublin, the barges would call in to other towns for fresh cargo to take back. There was always room for the beet that came up the Barrow from Carlow, or perhaps a load of malt barley to bring back to the Guinness Brewery. 'Carrying forty or fifty bags of malt weighing over twenty stone over your shoulder is no easy job,' counsels Tom, still feeling the weight.

Tom developed an intricate knowledge of the Irish waterways. The Barrow was lovely to go down 'but not so nice coming back – you'd have to winch your way through certain parts'. He has mastered the Erne, the Ballinasloe Canal, the Royal Canal and Lough Neagh. 'We made friends with all the lock-keepers and a lot of odd people along the way.'

The coming of the railways, and later the motor car, inevitably brought the age of the canals to an end. On 2 June 1960, Córas Iompair Éireann (CIE) closed the Grand Canal to navigation. Fortunately, the subsequent plan to convert the abandoned waterway into a motorway did not succeed.

Tom went on to work in the malt house in Rathangan, looking after the barley kept in stock for Guinness. 'It's gone now and I think they're developing it as a housing estate. But I was there a long time, shifting malt and turning it all day long.'

Today, Ireland's waterways have no commercial purpose but are still frequented by coarse fishermen, courting couples and old folk who remember the old days. 'I'm eighty-nine and I'm one of the last of the boat men now,' says Tom. 'I've one brother still alive and he's older than I am – he's ninety-three. He was a boatman too but he went to America in 1952.'

Joan and Tom were married in June 1945. They have enjoyed sixty-one years of marriage and have three sons and a daughter. As we prepare to leave, Tom throws his eyes at Joan and whispers to me, 'She was a great find.'

PADDY SCANLAN

Born 1926

Skipper & Lighthouse Keeper

Rosses Point, County Sligo

You might say Paddy Scanlan was born to the task. His father's people were amongst the principal seafaring families of Scattery Island in County Clare; his grandfather was one of the pilots who guided boats up and down the Shannon Estuary. Shortly after the First World War, the Commissioners of Irish Lights appointed Paddy's father, Patrick, to the position of keeper of the Sligo Lights at Rosses Point on the northwest coast of Ireland. His principal role was to keep an eye on the acetylene lights of the Oyster Island, Metal Man, Lower Rosses Point, Coney Island and Bomore Point lighthouses. Patrick was one of the two lighthouse keepers responsible for ensuring the Blackrock Lighthouse was charged every six weeks and that there was sufficient carbide in the lamps. There were two brothers from Coney Island who had the job of lighting the purchase with oil lamps on the channel up to Sligo, but when things got bad at the start of the Second World War, they went to America. 'One of them later became a cab driver in New York,' says Paddy.

The Scanlan family were given lodgings on Oyster Island and Paddy grew up on the island, the first son in a family of four girls and three boys. He has extremely fond memories of his childhood on the coast of County Sligo. They had goats for milk and chickens for eggs. Looking after such livestock was a task often given to the children. Every morning, a man called Josie Harn had the contract with Irish Lights to escort young Patrick and his siblings across the water to school in Rosses Point, throwing a wink at the Metal Man in Sligo Harbour as they passed. Their father was a big man with a tremendous passion for all things maritime. On the few occasions that he was home, he taught them how to hunt and fish on the island. They hunted rabbits on Coney Island and dug for cockles and razor fish on Lower Rosses, or lobsters and crab in the rocks around their home. With their air guns, they shot at thrushes and sometimes even 'the blackbird tasted really good'. In the evenings, the boys were often assigned the task of lighting the burner in the island's lighthouse.

In 1934, the Blackrock lighthouse was automated when the light was converted from oil to acetylene gas. Shortly afterwards, Patrick Scanlan was transferred to the lighthouse on Tuskar Rock, a dangerous low-lying rock six nautical miles northeast of Carnsore Point on the southeast coast of Ireland. The position involved staying on the rock itself for six weeks of every two months. His wife and five children stayed on the Irish mainland in a house outside Rosslare. On 2 December 1941, Patrick and William Cahill, his fellow assistant keeper, noticed that a British mine had washed up onto the rock. They kept a close eye on it all day but, tragically, just as Patrick opened the door of the lighthouse to see if it had drifted onwards, the mine detonated. Young Paddy was among several thousand who heard the explosion from the mainland. A lifeboat was rapidly dispatched from Rosslare and returned with the two injured men, but Patrick Scanlan died of his wounds early the next day. His fourteen-year-old oldest son remembers an older man approaching him soon afterwards. 'You are the head of the family now,' the man said.

However, for the young Sligo boy, there was only one thing to do. He joined the mail boat in Rosslare Harbour as a deck boy and was at sea until 1955. 'I was only fifteen when they took me on,' he laughs, 'but they needed bodies and they weren't checking for age. He subsequently saw action at the invasion of Sicily and the Battle of Anzio. His brother-in-law, also a merchant seaman, went down with the hospital ship *St David*, which was torpedoed in 1944.

Paddy left the merchant navy in 1948 and secured a post as assistant lighthouse keeper at the Blackrock Lighthouse, a famously desolate spot located some twelve miles off the Mullet Peninsula. One morning about six months later, Paddy looked out in great astonishment to see a 'blue funnel' of an ocean-going merchant ship passing by. He watched the ship's progress all day until it disappeared over the horizon. Paddy decided he'd had his fill of lighthouse keeping, resigned his post and rejoined the merchant navy. He remained with them until 1955 when he came back to Dublin and found employment as the skipper of one of the tug boats that guided the larger ships into Dublin Bay.

Paddy is married to Bernadette, a girl from Rosslare Harbour, and they have six children. The Scanlans live in Glasnevin on the northside of Dublin. The walls of their home are filled with pictures of tall ships, tea clippers and other sailing vessels collected by Paddy over the years. 'They think I'm mad having so many of them,' he says, 'but I don't mind because I can just look at them and I feel like I'm crossing the Indian Ocean again.'

ACKNOWLEDGEMENTS

We received help from an astonishing number of people in the making of this book.

Ruth Cunney and Hugo Jellett provided invaluable counsel, the 'Rosturk Proofers' excelled themselves and Nick Wilkinson conducted vital interviews with his customary deftness.

Thank you to Claire Rourke and all at Hodder Headline Ireland for their patience and fortitude. To Eneclann Ltd and the Tyrone Guthrie Centre at Annaghmakerrig for their ongoing support and to Karen Carty at Anú Design for her design.

The families and friends of the men and women we interviewed played a pivotal role and to them we say a massive thank you. We would also like to acknowledge the following for their sage words, scouting techniques, genteel manners and excellent cuisine.

Adam Green • Adam Monaghan • Aine O'Connor • Aine P. Kelly • Alan Philcox • Alice Boyle • Alice Power • Alicia Chawner • Alicia Parsons • Ana Wyndham Quin • Andy Cairns • Ann Healy • Andrew Davidson • Andrew Hewat • Angus Craigie • Anthony Ardee • Anthony Farrell • Anthony and Brooke Johns • Art Kavanagh • Arthur Johnson • Arthur Russell • Attracta Ryan • Becky Wilkinson • Ben Huskinson • Ben & Jessica Rathdonnell • Beth Ann Smith • Bill Cullen • Bill Howarth • Brian Donovan • Bridget Ryan • Caroline Hamilton • Catherine Anne Heaney • Cathy Curran • Cathy McCartney • Charles O'Brien • Charles O'Meara (Usual Place) • Chris & Moira Ryan • Ciara Cauldwell • Christy & Nellie Kelly • Clyne's Butchers, Ringsend • Colin Faraghy • Conor Walsh • Dave Kennedy • Dr David Kelly • Delma Furney • Denis Bergin Dominique Sinnott • Donal Fenelon • Durcan O'Hara • Earl & Countess of Dunraven • Eamon Bolger • Eddie Lenihan • Ed Somerville • Edwin & Nora Burgess • Elaine Kenelly • Eleanor Cullen • Eoghan Corry • Essie Conroy • Esther Whelan • Fred Hanna • Georgina Kelly • Gerry Mullins • Gussie Nagle • Harry & Nicola Everard • Harry & June Hodgson • Henry Hodgson • Hugh Murphy • Hugh Stewart • Isabell Smith • Isabella Nolan • Jamie Cahalane • Jed & Lucy Kelly • Jennifer Grimes • Jessica Slingsby • Jim McCabe • Jimmy Nagle • John Kennedy • John Nolan • John Reilly • John Rogers • Jonathan Stanistreet • Jos Donnelly • Justin & Jenny Green • Kieran & Linda Bergin • Leslie Burgess • Linda Farrell • Lizzie Meagher (Cara) • Lola O'Higgins • Louise Henry • Maebh Coyle • Marcus Williams • Mari Aymone Djerbi • Marie Twomey • Mark Onions • Martin Kelly • Mary Hoare Walsh • Mary Metcalfe • Matilda McBride • Matt & Georgie Tindal • Matthew & Alice Forde • Matthew Gallagher • Matthew Lloyd • Meike Blackwell • Michael & Clare fFrench-Davis • Michael Nolan • Michael Ryan • Micky Heffernan • Miriam Moore • Morgan Kavanagh • Nagles of Kilfenora • Nicola Morris • Noelle Moran • Nonee's Shop • Oisin & Aoife Nolan • Olaf Shiel • Paul Benney • Paddy Heaney • Paddy Knockton • Paddy Love • Pat Flynn • Pat Fouhy of Ballydaw • Patricia Scanlan • Patsey Murphy • Paul Devlin • Paul Manzor • Paul Smithwick • Pauline Bewick • Peter Keogh • Peter Mant • Peter Peart • Phil Burke (CAB, Nenagh) • Quentin Cooper • Richard & Louise Knatchbull • Richard & Jenny Pringle • Rita Nolan (*Within the Mullet*) • Sam & Phil Ware • Sarah-Beth Casey • Seamus & Emma Raben • Sean O'Reilly • Shane Jackson • Sheila Browne • Simon Pratt • Sir Richard Butler • Sonia Reynolds • Suzanne O'Hagan • Tom & Pam Butler • Tom & Sasha Sykes • Tom & Susi Lenox Conyngham • Tony Fenton • Tony Moreau • Trevor Gillespie • Siobhan Buchanan-Smyth • Sophie Gorman • Vaida Gasiunaite • Val Beamish • Wendy Walsh • William & Lesley Fennell.